PRAISE FOR

TAKE NOTHING WITH YOU

"I have known Skeeter since 1978. He is one of a kind. Having lived in Kenya the first nineteen years of his life, he knows what he is talking about.

At a Searching Together Gathering several years ago in Illinois, Skeeter gave three outstanding sessions: 'Into Africa,' 'Out of Africa,' and 'The Evils of Colonialism.' For years, I had serious reservations of the methods of traditional missions since the 1500s, especially the practice of imposing the missionary's culture on those being 'evangelized.'

This can be seen, for example, in the Presbyterian work among the Alaskan Tlingit Indians in 1877. Sheldon Jackson was the leader of this effort, and his goal was for these 'backward' Indians to ultimately come to the point where 'their highest ambition [would be] to build American homes, possess American furniture, dress in American clothes, be American citizens, and drop their stunted and dwarfed language for the liberal English.' In *Take Nothing With You*, Skeeter challenges such perverse goals, along with many others.

Take Nothing With You is a needful corrective to 600 years of well-intentioned, but very misguided, mission work. Somehow Jesus' words, 'take nothing with you,' have been lost in the shuffle of human traditions and human power structures.

"Skeeter has done what few have had the nerve to do and that is to tackle the sacred cow of 'Missions' in conversion Protestantism.

He, as a missionary kid and then as one well studied in African history is well qualified to bravely peel back the layers of western Christianity's role in 'missions' to reveal the real truth that it is not the true gospel being shared but soft colonialism.

One must persevere through what they may not like to hear to the second half of the book were Skeeter succinctly outlines why missions as we know it shouldn't exist and what should. Whether you agree or not with Skeeter, you will be better for having been challenged by his thoughts in this book.

"*Take Nothing With You* is an alarming and distressing look into the world of the Western Christian missionary, specifically in Africa.

Skeeter Wilson reveals—with a keen, gentle grace—the cruel and frequently brutal conduct of the white missionaries and the roles they have unwittingly played in enforcing the subjugation of Africans through the evangelizing of a whitewashed, Christian God.

Wilson emphasizes how the foundation and structure of the larger missionary movement is flawed, which in itself has resulted in procedures that have damaged not only missionaries themselves and their children but also has ultimately led to the complete breakdown of the cultural psyche of those Africans that they claim to save from hell. Rather than saving the African from hell, the missionaries of Western churches brought hell with them and continued the spinoff of an erroneous Christian culture that does not in any way resemble the teachings found in the Bible.

Take Nothing With You divulges the erroneous hand that these men and women of God have had in hindering the real message of the Christ—a message that is tender, deeply wise, and very true even today. A message that, unfortunately, almost two hundred years after the colonization and Christianization of Africa, has never really been heard nor shared.

– Najar Nyakio Munyinyi, Environmentalist
and Afri-Historian Researcher and Writer

Copyright © 2020 by Skeeter Wilson.

First Edition

Cover design and layout by Rafael Polendo (polendo.net). Cover image by storyblocks.com.

ISBN 978-1-938480-70-6

This volume is printed on acid free paper and meets ANSI Z39.48 standards.

Printed in the United States of America

 QUOIR

Published by Quoir
Orange, California

www.quoir.com

TAKE NOTHING WITH YOU

RETHINKING THE ROLE

OF MISSIONARIES

SKEETER WILSON

ACKNOWLEDGMENTS

This book is the result of a journey of a lifetime. There are so many who have shed light along my path at perfect moments. I have lost contact with too many, and many have passed on. To name a few: Mama Ruth, Pa Teasdale, Steve, Ruth, Anna, Esther, Yohanna Kamau, Dave Everett, Hassan Karama, Judy King, Steve Purdue, Mike Miller, Jon Zens, Bill Young, John Stringer, Mike Hagen, Jeff Testerman, Dave Roland, the Afterthoughts Writers, Baker Street Writers, Peter Kiarie, Oscar Chege, Trevor O'Hara, Mbaria wa Mbaria, Mordecai Ogada, Keith Giles, Mick Rineer, and most of all, my wife, Jacque Kae.

Not all are followers of the Way, but all have, in their own way, shown me the meaning and message of my faith. I am eternally grateful.

This book is for and because of them.

TABLE OF CONTENTS

FOREWORD

This is an extraordinarily honest book, so in keeping with that theme, I must disclose that the honor of writing this foreword hasn't been bestowed on me due to my expertise in the subject matter. I'd like to think that the reason is the author's and my unique mutual understanding of each other's baggage.

I am a black African, brought up in a practicing Christian home and partly educated in a church-run institution. I never felt the need to question the church until I enrolled in a church-run institution for my undergraduate studies. It was compulsory to take one or two credits in religious courses, which were taught with refreshing honesty, while being subject to pretty fundamentalist rules and regulations, which were enforced with missionary zeal. I saw black administrators aggressively enforcing *white* rules against various forms of adornment and culture, like the wearing of beads, the braiding of hair, and the playing of drums to accompany music. It was never expressly stated, but white was right.

Maybe the most disconcerting thing I saw was the spectacle of theology students (pastors in training) spending hours listening to audio recordings of American preachers as they strove to develop the same diction and accent. After graduation in zoology and completion of my advanced degrees in wildlife ecology, I met a familiar white-is-right tone in the conservation sector, which led to many battles that made me suffer terrible self-doubt because my professional field totally accepted so many conservation injustices that I personally considered anathema.

A conservation writer, Gatu Mbaria, and I met in 2015 and decided to pen a book about these issues, and after over a year of consistent rejection of our ideas, we virtually met Skeeter and sent him our manuscript. I wasn't optimistic. Our blunt portrayal of racial prejudice in conservation had been rejected by all the black Africans we shared it with. What were the odds that a white man would see our point? He saw it instantly and took it up.

When we finally met in person, we instantly became old friends. I'm always moved by Skeeter's relentless focus on truth and unwillingness to accept prevailing dogma, be it social, religious, or political. This resonated deeply in my life where I saw the influence of white is right all around me. Christianity and the gospel was brought to my country (Kenya) by missionaries, and it is accepted to be the good news of the Kingdom of God.

What escapes many people, particularly in the missionaries' countries of origin, is that when something is considered *good*, it is impossible for the secondary recipient who accepts this message not to consider the person that had it first to be *better* than him. This is a simple step of logic, yet generation after generation of missionaries has failed to acknowledge, much less address, this basic problem of principle.

Skeeter is still the only person I know to have addressed this issue expressly, and the only one to clearly see the link between missionaries and the acceptance that white is right in so many spheres of African lives.

There is pain in this book, and any perceptive reader will see that it wasn't an easy one to write. One would have to be extremely naïve to even imagine addressing these matters without any trauma, and the strength of this book lies in the way Skeeter demonstrates to us that trauma is a normal part of growth. There is the frustration of the numerous departures therein from familiar people, places, and paths that sometimes feels like suffering. However, life itself is full of twists and turns, so the departures are a sure sign of a soul that knows its orientation and doesn't deviate from it.

Skeeter describes a series of occurrences that he considered to be his signs of the influence of a Higher Power in his life. I have often described Skeeter Wilson as one of the very few genuine Christians I know. As a person, there is very little in my experience with the church that could inspire me to call myself a believer. However, when I look at how I met Skeeter, how much we have shared, and how much he has influenced my life, I have gained more than belief, I have gained knowledge.

– **Dr. Mordecai Ogada**, Nanyuki, Kenya, January 2020,
co-author with John Mbaria of *The Big Conservation Lie*

THE GATE

G iant metal hinges carried the ancient wooden planks of the gate as it swung back and forth across the dirt and stone driveway to the house. Somehow over the years, the gate faithfully groaned as us kids rode it the full 180 degrees while we dreamed our childhood dreams. The youngest of five children, I was the last to dream from that perch.

Inside the enclosure over which the gate stood centurion, was the setting for an idyllic childhood. An orchard with lemons, figs, and apples and a garden filled with vegetables that flourished between the two planting seasons in the Kenyan highlands. Between the orchard and the garden was a fence burdened with passion fruit vines and grapes.

The house was a Dutch Colonial two-story constructed with cut stone walls and a gambrel roof. Surrounding the house was a carefully manicured lawn with a variety of flowers including poinsettias, carnations, bougainvillea, tropical orchids, African lilies, and birds-of-paradise, to name a few. A tall loquat tree stood on the east end of the house overlooking a rose garden fed from the gray water effluent of the house.

And the sound of the gate—old metal scraping against well-worn metal—would serve as a descanting alert to everyone in the enclosure of a visitor, friend or stranger.

It is hard to imagine a more perceptively perfect place for the children of missionaries to spend their formative years. How I loved to walk barefoot in the garden, weeding, planting, and harvesting, forming a lifelong love of gardening.

My bedroom was upstairs at the east end of the house. When needed, I would climb out onto the roof and into the branches of the loquat tree and down to the ground. I'd crawl under the fence to avoid the noise of the gate alerting others of my escape. And I often needed a way of escape throughout my childhood.

There was a malignancy in the house, a house filled with anger, ironclad control, sexual abuse, and the fragility of mental illness. It was a house where eye contact was often carefully avoided, a life of tiptoeing to avoid irrational anger or triggering emotional breakdowns. Emotions, opinions, and the questions of youth were too dangerous to venture. There was no place to safely grow.

When the anger and emotional fragility left the house, to do their bidden missionary work, a gray cloud lifted. Children played and laughed and had over the few friends they could psychologically muster, always keeping a wary ear for the sound of the gate.

The epitome of the household was daily devotions, a time when something from the Bible was read, or something from a book about stories of the Bible. Devotions ended after each member of the household shared what they had gotten out of the reading and a prayer in which everyone made their offerings scripted from a list of printed prayer requests and petitions for better understanding of the Bible. There was not a more toxic and dangerous time in the house. No question dared go beyond parameters guided by the dogma of the enveloping missionary world, and the interpretive genius of a deceased but ever-present grandfather. It was not a time to think. It was a time to submit.

Outside the wooden gate was a world both familiar and dangerous. My parents were respected missionaries and appeared to be highly regarded among those in the African church. Countless lives were saved directly or indirectly through their ministry. My father could build or fix anything. Anything. He was the manager of the Kijabe mission station, for most of the years that I grew up, responsible for roads, electric generators, and the station budget. Weekends were spent visiting different churches, preaching, and calling the lost to salvation.

There was a missionary boarding school on the station. It was a place where, from several surrounding countries, the children of missionaries who had answered the call of God to fulfill their vocation would be sent nine months out of the year to be raised by others. This apparently was what God wanted. Many a child of missionaries suffered in quiet anguish, because to complain was to reject their parents' calling by God.

Beyond the mission station, surrounding it on three sides, were the magnificent forests of the Kenyan highlands, the primary homeland of the Agikuyu people. Now, years later, those forests have been cut down and the land turned into farmland, but in my childhood, the forests were magnificent and endless, where adventures and misadventures marked the happiest moments of my childhood. The station was situated on a shelf of land halfway down the Great Rift Valley and on the fourth and final side was abutted by a one-thousand-foot drop to the beginning of the vast savannah of the Maasai lands. It was a stunningly beautiful place.

Beyond the mission station there were also skepticism, unbelief, and questions. There were people angry at missionaries for imposing a Western God and benefiting by—and even partnering with—colonial expansionism in its century-old quest to subdue Africa for the economic benefit of the West. There was a deep dichotomy among the Africans I grew up with as to the nature (good or evil) of missionaries and their God.

Recently, one of my sisters reminded me of conversations we had over fifty years ago together on that gate that stood guard over the enclosure in which we were partly raised. Neither one of us remembered the specifics of those conversations, but we both remembered what they were about and the questions they raised. In many ways, both of us have lived our life seeking, on our separate paths, our own answers to those questions.

Even as children, there were two things we were certain of:

First, we were certain the Christianity that we grew up in—at the station and inside our gated home—was not true Christianity. We did not see that missionary endeavors were very loving to Africans. We did not think that being white know-it-alls benefited Africans, or anyone. We knew very well that the perfectly manicured missionary façade we were made a part of fell apart within our home. We did not think that our house, with its cut stone walls and gambrel roof, was really the testimony that our parents claimed it was, that showing the material benefits of being Christians was really the message of the Jesus who said, "Foxes have holes, and birds have nests, but the Son of Man has no place to lay His head." It seemed to us that the testimony of the station we grew up in was the mirror opposite to the message of the Christ.

Second, we were certain that we would make every effort to learn what the message of the Christ really was, and that we would become a part of an authentic faith. We were certain that in so doing, we would change the world for the better.

In my early twenties, I made an outline for a book I wanted to write about missionaries. I kept it in my files for years. The book was to be titled *Building Roads*. In it, I hoped to explore different types of missionary endeavors. In my mind at that time, there was a "good" and a "destructive" missionary model. My outline for my book reflected that idea.

In the intervening years of my life, my faith has been filled with doubt, anger, disbelief, and wonder, a journey that anyone who has lived a life exploring the spiritual will understand. I have never fully stopped looking for the authentic faith that my sister and I talked about while swinging on our big wooden gate. Time is a good and sometimes cruel teacher. With each decade, I had to discard sections of my outline for *Building Roads* until, at last, I abandoned the premise altogether. I am glad now that I never wrote that book.

Of course, there will be new lessons learned and shifts in my perspective, if I am permitted to live additional decades, but the book I write now reflects my perspective, in this decade of my life, on missionaries. For the most part, I will focus on three things central to the modern concept of missions: education, culture, and message.

I do not for a moment doubt the sincerity and good intentions of most missionaries around the world, especially in the Africa where I grew up. Nor do I doubt the sincerity that drives them to believe that they are fulfilling a divine calling. But I do very much doubt that the missionary movement faithfully reflects the teachings and examples of the Christ who is the purported subject of their message and purpose.

For now, my perspective is that, regardless of motives and intentions, the best thing that a missionary—individually and in society—can do is to simply go home. What follows is an explanation of the major reasons behind this belief.

CHAPTER 1

MY MOTIVATION

Considering the diversity of my friends and acquaintances in the United States and in Africa, I anticipate a wide range of reactions to this book. Some might wonder why I am wasting my time writing about the obvious; others will take offense at my characterizations of the missionary movement. A few, perhaps, will find my reasoning persuasive.

Early in 2019, when my battle with cancer entered round two, in between the less than lovely treatments and periods of recuperation that followed them, I chose to spend the time and energy I had writing the articles that were the basis of this book. Various segments, as I wrote, were posted on social media. I posted them, in part, to gauge reactions, and in part, because I did not know if I would have, ultimately, the time or energy to produce this book.

The content of this book is the result of a lifetime of struggling over the key topics presented herein.

In recent years, various missionaries and children of missionaries have sent me a link to an article that was published in the 2014 January–February issue of *Christianity Today* entitled "The Surprising Discovery About Those Colonialist, Proselytizing Missionaries." The motive, it seems, in sending the link was to demonstrate, to a naysayer like me, how much good has been done by the very missionaries that

I have decried as being irreparably flawed and harmful both in the societies in which they work and to the very nature of the gospel itself. It is an article that uses what seems to be a good analysis to point out a set of unintended, so-called positive consequences created by a very specific brand of missionary, conversion Protestants, that are not funded by any state.

Loosely speaking, conversion Protestants derived themselves from evangelical Protestants. They comprise about one-third of the estimated half a million missionaries worldwide. The remaining missionaries are mainline Protestants, Roman Catholics, and sectarians. The distinction, as the word "conversion" suggests, is that these Protestants are looking for a profession of faith—a response to an alter call, for instance—as has been popularized in Western Christianity since the Second Great Awakening, (roughly 1820–1850). Non–conversion Protestants are generally more focused on education and humanitarian aid.

Since the subjects of the *Christianity Today* article are the same brand of missionaries that I grew up with, as the son of conversion Protestant missionaries, I will address most of my remarks toward them. However, I submit that many of the same criticisms apply to the broader spectrum of all missionary societies and foreign aid organizations, be they religious or not.

It was during my attempts to address the content of the article that this book truly began to take shape. What I will address will go beyond the scope of the article, but I will return to it from time to time. I certainly encourage those interested to find and read the article. If, however, one chooses not to read the article, the context I provide hopefully will suffice.

I found two factually incorrect assertions made in the article. I doubt they originate from the study behind the article.

First, contrary to the article's claims, early missionaries of the modern missionary movement, especially Protestant missionaries from the United States and Britain, were, in fact, trying to spread Western ideas of capitalism among their converts. This was not unintentional. The famous David Livingstone captured the imagination of the early movement with his vision that the best way to end slavery in Africa was to introduce what became famously known as the "three Cs"— commerce, Christianity, and civilization. Commerce, in that era, was understood as capitalism. Most early missionaries were captivated by Livingstone's argument for the moral imperative of capitalism to end slavery.

Second, it is not accurate to imply that non-state-funded conversion Protestants were not beholden to colonialism. In fact, just the opposite is true. It was at the invitation and under the direction of colonial powers that missionaries were given passage, properties, areas of "mission," and conditions—which will be described in more detail later. The few colonial powers that resisted allowing conversion Protestants into their domains were ultimately persuaded to do so by other colonial powers.

The conditions upon which the early conversion Protestants were invited (allowed), I will point out, are a key issue. And I submit that the very definition of what a missionary, then or today, does or should do is defined by colonialist intentions, not scripture. A bold statement, perhaps, but I hope to defend it as we continue.

Early missionaries could protest the colonial powers all they wanted, but in the end, they were still doing exactly what those governments wanted of them.

The *Christianity Today* article touts that countries where these conversion Protestants had a significant presence have achieved a higher education attainment and, by consequence, more stable governments, more progressive women's rights, more economic stability, and lower mortality rates.

All these achievements may seem noble (I assure you they are not seen as noble in the slightest in the minds of many in the colonialized world), but none of them is an objective of the Christ or part of the message of Christ. All of them are, instead, objectives of Western civilization. I can hear the protests already, but I contend that this only proves the effectiveness of the conversion Protestants in disseminating Western ideas. But it does little to demonstrate the fidelity of conversion Protestants to the Christ, nor does it point to an effectiveness in transmitting the Christian message itself.

As I wrote these essays, my original intention was to make this a semi-academic work, with the hope that, when I was well enough to do so, I would go back and reference my sources. However, I have decided against presenting this book in a highly annotated way. These are my organic thoughts that are an accumulation of reading, a decade of interviews with elderly African men and women, and my own experiences in the missionary world. I have chosen to keep these only slightly modified from the original posts as I presented them on social media. I think this has a more personal feel.

It is my heart on paper, and I think it is best to leave it as such.

I have paid minimal attention to order. Some chapters naturally follow each other, some stand alone, some are similar themes from a different perspective of what was presented in previous chapters. Hopefully, some of you will see a kind of beauty in the random nature of these essays.

There is always much more to say on a subject like this, and perhaps in the future, I will say more in another collection of writings.

I hope this is has been enough to demonstrate my motivation for and style of presenting the themes in this book.

CHAPTER 2

A BRIEF HISTORY

For those unfamiliar with the history of missionaries, there are three generally recognized so-called Christian missionary movements.

The first movement was in early post-Constantine Christianity (fourth century). This movement spread generally into Europe and is largely responsible for the Christianization of Europe.

The second movement occurred along with the first colonial expansion into the Americas, the Far East, and island isolates.

The third movement occurred along with colonization of Africa, or the Scramble for Africa. This movement was not limited to Africa; it also involved conversion Protestants retracing many of the Catholic strongholds of the previous missionary movement.

Of course, there have been missionaries in operation at some level through all post-Constantine Christianity, but these three movements represent periods of more concerted efforts.

Before these three movements, Christianity spread somewhat into southern Europe but mostly into Asia, India, and throughout much of Africa. This early spread occurred in a more organic way and does not fit the characteristics of the three missionary movements I have described.

The earliest expansions of believers, before the fourth century, differed in several significant ways from later missionary efforts, but the most profound difference is that the earliest expansions of believers were not remotely associated with the expansion of empire. Quite to the contrary, the Roman Empire, through much of those early years, were in direct opposition to the message of the Christ and at times attempted to violently bring the message and its followers to an end.

CHAPTER 3

BAGGAGE

I am writing this chapter from the point of view of a generally Protestant perspective. I no longer consider myself a part of the Protestant tradition, but I was raised in it (more Baptistic), was trained in it, and it is within the perspective of the conversion Protestant missionaries talked about in the *Christianity Today* article to which I largely respond. Fair enough?

If you have ever wondered how New Testament doctrine came to be doctrine, the basic traditional Protestant rule is based on rules of textual interpretation. For those in the Catholic and Orthodox traditions, the process is similar, but the final interpretation and application of passages is in the hands of tradition and central authorities rather than left to individual investigation. Let me correct that last statement. Those older traditions also encourage individual investigation. However, the difference lies in the authority of traditional church dogma as opposed to authority in the individual or local communities.

For the traditional Protestant, the rule of interpretation follows like this: a teaching must first have been taught by Jesus and then demonstrated in the epistles. Voila, doctrine!

Now that you know it—if you didn't before—know that it is a rule that should be rescinded (as my Catholic and Orthodox friends will tell you). It creates a lot of trouble trying to determine what, exactly, Jesus taught and what, exactly, is being demonstrated in the epistles, what, exactly, is the Bible and why, if the epistles carried such weight in validating the teachings of Jesus, did it take over three hundred years to assemble them—and these are just some of the simpler issues created by the rule of interpretation.

Why do I say all this? Well, to impress you with my memory of my doctrines class in the seventies is number one. However, I would like to mention a little something that Jesus said in the book of Matthew, when he sent His disciples out, to heal the sick and proclaim the good news. Roughly paraphrased it says:

> Don't carry any gold, silver, or copper in your money belts. Don't take any baggage—no extra shirts, sandals, or staff— for the work (healing and sharing the gospel) will earn your provisions. When you go into a town or village, look for a worthy person to stay with until you leave. If you are not welcomed, then leave that town and shake the dust off your feet as a testimony against them.

These instructions are repeated at least two times, and possibly four times, in the four Gospels. If these can be demonstrated in the epistles (according to Protestant tradition), then the entire missionary world is in contradiction to its teacher. Perhaps Protestant missionaries should take heed.

The convenient escape clause, of course, which makes establishing doctrine so awful, is that for every example I give of this in the epistles, if you don't want to agree, you simply deny the example, and thus throw out the teaching of the Jesus you claim to follow.

Now I will give two examples of this teaching in the epistles.

First, remember when Peter and John met the lame man in the book of Acts? Peter's response to the beggar's request was, "Silver and gold have I none, but such as I have, I give to you."

It is incredibly unlikely that neither Peter nor John had any possession of silver or gold. It is far more likely that they knew they might meet poor people on their way to the temple and so left their silver and gold at home.

Both of these men had learned the practice of a common purse while traveling with Jesus (another interesting part of what Jesus practiced that is again demonstrated in the epistles), but the likelihood that such a purse was empty is not nearly as likely as that they, from practice, simply did not carry money with them when they went out. It seems clear, from various sources, that Peter was a well-connected person with some wealthy land-owning relatives, not one who lacked for money. No, when he went out, he "[did] not bring any gold or silver or copper to take with [him] in [his] belt."

Second, if you have ever followed the journeys of the Apostle Paul as outlined primarily in the book of Acts, you might have run into a curiosity in his destinations. Why would he skip over several major towns and end up in less significant towns to engage in his wandering ministry?

Everywhere he went, he stayed with someone who he met when he arrived, who welcomed him in and usually begged him not to leave. Several times, these were wealthy women engaged in the trades, possibly because Paul (a tent maker) was also in the trades professionally. I won't do your homework for you but look at the language when Paul came to a town and found "some worthy person and [stayed] at the house until [he left]." Neither Jesus nor Paul stayed where they were not welcomed, nor stayed long where they were.

Doctrine!

Ultimately, approaching texts to establish dogma is a bad idea and as often as not creates division among God's people. I think, however, the teachings and example of the Christ, based on His own instructions, are given for us to follow. It seems that the least we can do as people of faith is to focus on those teachings and examples above everything else. Our life should be a journey, not an establishment and defense of dogma.

Let's contrast this example and teaching of the Christ with a man who is, for many, the father of modern missions, William Carey. There is a lot to admire about the man. He died about fifty years before the so-called Golden Age of Missions and was not party to a lot of the evil that I see still emanating from that period. But I do want to point out the troublesome precedent set by Carey and others.

It is said that Carey spent thirty years in India before he saw his first convert. Compare that to Jesus, a wandering man with no place to lay His head at night, and Paul, who spent at most two to three months in any given place where he was welcomed. The exceptions to Paul's short stays included his year-and-a-half stay in Corinth and three years in Ephesus—both are understandable in their context.

In the places Paul wasn't welcomed, he did not stay. None of Paul's efforts resemble the thirty years of Carey, or the multiple years of the modern missionary. Of prime importance to Paul was that his converts "know nothing among them except Christ and Him crucified." Paul's role model, it seems, was Jesus. Jesus is the example that pitifully few people who call themselves missionaries take seriously.

None, absolutely none, of the damage by modern missionaries could possibly have occurred if missionaries followed the example of the One whose name they attribute to themselves. Upon what credible basis do people leave one culture and go to another culture and live where they are not welcomed (or not invited by a worthy person with whom to stay) and stay anyway until they win over enough locals to start a church with a message inevitably so diluted by the clash of culture that irreparable damage is done to the objective of leaving nothing among them other than Christ and Him crucified?

Missionaries have wandered so far from the source that it seems they forget there is a source in the first place.

Schools? Bibles? What, pray tell, are these things for? And the ability to read? Where is this found in the teaching and example of the Christ? How did Jomo Kenyatta (not a hero of mine) say it? Something like, "They gave us a Bible and taught us to pray. When we opened our eyes, we had their Bible and they had our land." This is spot on.

Perhaps the reason to go is medicine? After all, Jesus is the great healer, why not go heal the sick?

When I think of this issue, I am reminded of my all-time favorite short (non)fiction story, "The Things They Carried," by Tim O'Brien. I am not nor have I ever been a warrior. Spiritual, physical, and intellectual barriers have kept that from ever happening. But O'Brien writes of all the physical and mental baggage one carried as an American soldier in the Việt Nam war. Physical wars require such baggage.

And this is what I see when missionaries carry their own baggage with them to another culture. They have added a physical component to a spiritual kingdom—physical things, mental things. Their weapons are often disguised as gifts and talents intended as good works in an awkward example of compassion. They look at the good works of Jesus, who took nothing on His journey, and try to interpret that into a physical, organized solution—the things they carry. It is not necessary, it is not expedient, it is not the example to follow nor follows the instructions given for those who believe.

Here, instead, are the instructions the Christ gave—in the book of Matthew—for being a missionary: no money, no baggage, don't stay where you aren't welcomed.

Honestly, I believe the word "missionary" should be eradicated from the vocabulary of a follower of the Christ. It is a word born in colonialism with no real foundation in the teachings of Christ except for a few cherry-picked verses that are ripped out of their contexts.

Go and do likewise, or don't go. If modern missionaries truly base their doctrines on a better or broader source of some Biblical principle over and above the words of the Christ himself, please elucidate me.

CHAPTER 4

THE SACRED COW

In the chapter "Motivation," I mentioned that education is one of the so-called achievements of missionaries that is touted in the article "The Surprising Discovery About Those Colonialist, Proselytizing Missionaries."

I will assume that most will agree with me that education is one of the West's most sacred cows. For the West, the theoretical purpose of education has been to maintain democracy. Since the industrial revolutions in the West, however, the practical purpose of education has become to produce a useful and compliant workforce (a discussion in itself). This motive has, in many ways, superseded all other motives. For a conversion Protestant, the additional and, in theory, greater purpose is to make it possible for everyone to be able to read the Bible in their own language.

Ultimately, the Western mind seems to believe that every problem can be solved with just a little more education—Western-style education, of course.

Every civilization has methods of education, some far more sophisticated than others, but education and its delivery is the essence of any civilization. If you kill the educational system of a culture, the culture will not survive. That statement should be uncontestable, or as the Puritans used to say, self-evident.

I will save until later some of the problems of the Western world's ideas of education and, more especially, the problem of education that is exported from one civilization to another. For now, however, let's stay focused on the role of missionaries in education and their motives.

Here I quote from the article: "While missionaries came to colonial reform through the back door, mass literacy and mass education were more deliberate projects—the consequence of a Protestant vision that knocked down old hierarchies in the name of 'the priesthood of all believers.' If all souls were equal before God, everyone would need to access the Bible in their own language. They would also need to know how to read."

So, there you have it. According to the article the missionaries' motivation to educate is that all newly converted believers can read the Bible.

Interesting, indeed, since believers in the first several centuries after the Christ had an almost identical perceived illiteracy rate as Africans did before colonialism. In truth, Africans were not illiterate before colonialism—that is a Western myth—but I am referring here to *accepted* statistics.

No one in those early centuries after the Christ had access to a Bible, as we know it, because it did not exist until the fourth century, and even in the fourth century, it was remarkably different from what we now call the Bible.

There is no evidence of a mass education campaign in the early church. How on earth did they survive, thrive, and grow? How did they have any concept of a "priesthood of all believers" without missionaries to educate them? In fact, considering the conversation of Jesus and Nicodemus and the Apostle Paul's statements about his own education—"I count everything as a loss in comparison to the value of knowing the Christ …"—one would think a better argument can be made against education than for it. But even that argument is in the Bible—which did not exist, as such, in those first centuries of believers in the Christ.

So, the question becomes this. What exactly is accomplished when one culture goes and educates another culture to teach them to read and learn a book that has been translated and traditionalized through the cultural lens of the educators? Perhaps some strange and confusing ideas of God; a lily-white Jesus; bastardized concepts of the church, worship, salvation, and the meaning of the Christ?

Paul, I think, would be absolutely appalled at what the modern missionary is doing with education. May I dare say, he would call it a false gospel, as he did in Galatians when he confronted those who wanted others to conform to their culture. When he said, in his first letter to the Corinthians, "I decided to know nothing among you except Christ and Him Crucified," clearly, he was mistaken? Did he not understand that those Greek and Italian converts, who knew nothing of the Hebrew Bible, needed an education in reading Hebrew and understanding all the promises that led up to the Christ? He, it seems, was foolish enough to think that people could simply accept or reject the Christ's message and then he could simply walk away (or be carried out after a stoning)—all without an education program!

There is no precursor to Paul's message, there is no burden put on the believer other than to follow the Christ. There is no mandate on circumcision, medicine, buildings, or education. These are all Western traditionalism, and they have nothing to do with the gospel or the intended message of a believer.

Today's missionaries seem to think that they know better. They have learned to build culturally inappropriate buildings that separate young, malleable minds from parents and their parents' traditions and to inoculate these young minds (under the banner of Western enlightenment) with a good dosage of individualism, thereby keeping them from ever fully returning to their parents' world. Then the missionaries give their tutees the white Jesus and a translation of a translation through a Western lens that bears little resemblance to their own culture (which they are by then cut off from anyway). Is this what is considered an improvement on Paul's method?

If Paul had only used modern methods, he could have brought the whole world under the single banner of Hebrew culture. Oh, yes! Now I remember—Paul, in his letter to the Galatians, castigated (or at least suggested castration for) believers who behaved like this. If bringing believers under the cultural banner of Israel was considered a false gospel in Galatia, how much more of a false gospel is it to bring believers in Africa under the culture banner of the west?

Later, I intend to mention what Christ taught about the manner and message of the disciples. It is shocking to me that modern missionaries seem to ignore what their Christ has to say, but they can accept, instead, what their mission board has to say with minimal crises of conscience.

Perhaps I have pushed too far too soon. I can hear cries of "Unfair!" from both ends of the spectrum. I want to point out, however, that no matter what you think is a minimal or necessary addition to the message—be it education, medicine, famine relief, water systems— you are adding something to a message that Paul was determined to let stand on its own. Any minimal addition is the proverbial camel's nose under the tent. One simply can't add a little culture to a message without adding the entire culture. That is, in part, what the circumcision debate in the book of Acts and Galatians was all about.

Yes, I know about the many texts, such as the Sermon on the Mount, that point to the poor, needy widows, and orphans. But I dare you to find a verse that says the way to aid the least of these is to give them over to a Christian organization that will be certain to channel its funds appropriately—some of it to the needy. In fact, the entire idea of organizational help is a Western construct with devastating effects on cultures that are not so dedicated to individualism. There is a big difference between organizing ones giving to the poor (as Paul did) and giving gifts to a charitable organization.

One more swipe at the education peddled by missionaries: Why, pray tell, if the motive of the Western Protestant is Biblical literacy, do they teach everything else? Why do they teach about the finding of America, those "heroic" voyagers from Europe who discovered the New World—which apparently did not exist before they stumbled across it. It would seem their primary goal is not education; it is, instead, reeducation.

Biblical education (whatever that means) quickly becomes a sideline, useful for raising funds.

Do not protest too much. I am judging based on actions. The reality is cultures that the missionary does not understand—and often considers sinful or demonic or based in witchcraft—are met with education. Education is the antidote in the Western mind for everything of which he is ignorant. And not any education, mind you, Western education. Education, not Christ.

But can't we use Western-style education, or any education style, for that matter, to lead people to Christ? Absolutely not! If you haven't figured this out by now, please read on.

Colonialism wanted missionaries precisely because they are Western education machines. The primary reason missionaries were invited into the bosom of the colonial structure at the turn of the last century (the Golden Age of Missions) is because colonial governments and neocolonial powers knew from the previous two colonial movements exactly what happens when one sends in the missionaries. And it worked perfectly. It worked for the colonial governments and the now despot governments that followed them. And I maintain that it destroyed the message of the cross in the process.

In the National Archives in Nairobi, I found notes from colonial provincial governors outlining their monthly meetings. One report submitted at each meeting was on the progress of missionary work. Given top billing in this report was education. The willingness of the colonial powers to grant additional areas of work to a mission society was based on that society's ability to establish schools in the areas that they were assigned. Any unwillingness on the part of a mission society to educate and the missionary endeavor would not last long in the colony. There were always plenty of other missionary societies to choose from.

Some have argued that the fact that colonial aggression and the major missionary movements happened at the same time is merely coincidental. Those who feel this way should take a journey to the archives of the countries where their favorite missionary endeavors occurred during the colonial period. They should take the time to read the level of collusion. Indeed, the ultimate motives differed between the missionaries and the colonial overlords. But the records are quite clear that the modern missionary movements and colonial expansion were anything but coincidental.

Why is it that missionaries never question the educational system they have established? Where is the literature where they have discussed more culturally appropriate methods—or where they explored teaching the gospel through the existing educational system of the cultures that they ministered to?

Better yet, where are the articles that question the basis of education as the work of missionaries at all?

The answer is simple: the educative mandate came not from God; it came, instead, from colonialism. It was easy for missionaries to justify this, as they too believed that the wretched heathen needed to be elevated to a higher level (in the earlier years that meant white man's civilization). Missionaries who were appalled at the system were removed, and the missionaries who remained became the company of the compliant. Like it or not, when it comes to education and the missionary, this is the truth.

Within a few years after encountering the colonial invasion (which is what it was), the Gikuyu people sent some of their brightest young people—among them Jomo Kenyatta—overseas to get a Western education. Their mission was to receive a Western education and bring it back to the people. The Gikuyu could see there was a lot of power in the education of the West. When these young people returned, they set up Gikuyu-run schools all over their lands. Unfortunately, they adopted some of the structure of Western education, but nevertheless, they were still self-educating within their own culture. One would think that the colonial government would have been happy and praised the natives in their enterprise and that the missionaries would have been delighted that they could return to their first directive, the gospel. But no. The government outlawed any native-run education and turned the Gikuyu schools over to—you guessed it—a missionary agency. And praise God, the relationship between the colony and the missionary grew ever stronger.

It was and is not education, per se, that matters to the colonial, neocolonial, and the missionary. It was specifically Western education that mattered/matters because it separates the student from his or her culture and ensures that they can never truly go home (or maintain continuity with their past). Not ever.

CHAPTER 5

HEALING

I suppose, considering my intended subject, that there is a bit of a delicious irony that while writing this I am facing what is often considered a dreaded and very possibly fatal disease. I am equally blessed by those who offer sincere prayers on my behalf and those who wish me well without enjoining divine healing. A part of me is reflected in both the believers and non. I deeply love and respect you no matter where you are in this journey of life. In addition, I am married to a physician, whom I love and admire, and I yearn to follow her example of strength, love, and compassion. She has traveled the world practicing medicine, and I would have it no other way.

One small disclaimer before I continue. I have dedicated a considerable part of my life to thinking about and studying education, at least philosophically. I have, on the other hand, just as judiciously avoided studying medicine and healing. I am currently under the care of those who do study both traditional Western and naturopathic medicine. I am grateful for them but still feel disinclined to spend too much energy on the subject on a personal level. I claim no special insight into the philosophy, art, or science of medicine.

I stated in the previous chapter that education is a sacred cow of the Western world, not just any education, but specifically Western education. This is equally true of medicine. It is also equally true that missionaries have been one of the most effective vehicles for establishing medical clinics and hospitals in the non-Western world. Colonial powers knew this well, and it is the second most important reason that colonial expansion wanted missionaries at the tip of the spear.

This is an amazingly untouchable subject for all parties involved.

It will subdue the most unrelenting and miscreant native in any society. Sooner or later, even the most errant natives will step inside the stone and concrete castle of Western medicine and, in so doing, they will immediately be forced to reimagine who they are in the world.

They can never again be who they were before entering that clinic or hospital door. They enter beneath the white cross on the lintel and carry their sick loved ones down each corridor filled with messages and images of a European Christ. They may not have entered to encounter this God, but the power of the association of this God implicit in their loved one's healing will forever be entwined with the healing itself. What amazes me is that, for most missionaries, this association is seen as a good thing. Mind you, it is particularly important to missionaries that the God associated with this moment of healing be their own special brand of God.

Even the most grudging atheists have admitted to me that medicine is at least one thing that missionaries do well. It isn't, but I'll get to that.

Besides, my unbelieving friends, you all have been doing your own version of missionary work since the fifties, and you're screwing it up just as bad. I am grateful that your arguments have challenged my faith and made me better for it—I love you guys too—but I'm addressing missionaries here. I also love missionaries, and I deeply respect their compassion, but I take exception to their vocation, not themselves individually. They are not my enemies. If they were, this conversation would be completely different, perhaps less confrontational.

Back to healing.

Medicine is the foot in the door that wins the argument every time. Of course, you can't expect a compassionate, loving person to see such needless yet curable sickness and not feel compelled to help. Medicine is the one piece of baggage about which no decent person can argue against a God-fearing missionary carrying with them.

I must not be decent, because I say to the missionary that when you picked up that medicine bag, you forever poisoned the message that your missionary endeavor was designed to deliver. You are now bearing witness to the gospel of the Western world rather than to the Christ. Team Colonialization (or whatever despot or struggling nation you have associated with) wins the match, and you are the lead striker (a little *futebol* lingo).

Someone may object and point out that Jesus was, himself, the Great Healer! One can't be Jesus, one may reason, but perhaps I can offer what I do have. I may feel that I cannot offer hope if I do not include healing and compassion with it.

Did I mention that the one called Jesus was not a doctor? He did not carry a medicine bag. He did not found any medical society. He did not set up a single medical clinic. There was no patient list. There was no follow-up care. There was no medical practice, art, or science at all. And every indication is that all those healed were no less subject to the same frailties of life that all others faced. The meaning of the bodily healing the Christ did is not to be found in the healing itself.

When it comes to the stories of the healings performed by the Christ, it seems we have at least three basic choices: either none of the stories is true and all are myth or folklore; or perhaps they are explained by inner or self-healing—a spiritual placebo, if you will; or the healings were extraordinary events to be called miracles. And I am going to assume that by virtue of being a missionary, one who has answered the call would be most inclined to believe (or at least teach) the doctrine of miracles.

Jesus did not carry a medicine bag—he was not in the medicine business. Healing that comes from a medicine bag cannot be compared to healing with empty hands. The two types of healing are not made of the same stuff; there is no direct connection to make.

The miracles of Christ established who He was and authenticated His message. The problem of using Western medicine to authenticate the message of Christ is it does no more than to ensure that the message cannot be distinguished from Western culture.

THE CONTEXT OF HEALING

Healing from a medicine bag is, or should be, a compassionate and very human act. I make no disparaging comments about it. Medicine is rooted in the human experience, and as with all human endeavors, it comes with its own special baggage. Sometimes this baggage comes in the form of concrete boxes that climb like a religious edifice into the sky. But the medicine and its baggage are always earthly, physical, and entirely human.

Almost without exception, every culture has medicine in some form. These cultures have developed, through a history of their own experience, the lines between the art, mystery, and science of healing.

Medical practitioners are, almost without exception, among the best and the brightest of their cultures. Every culture understands that the balance of life and death is held by virtue of their medicine. And the impulse to associate their practices with their deity or deities is almost inescapable. Healing is both an act of compassion and, often, the hope to delay our journey beyond the veil of this life.

Contained in the medicine bag of every culture is the culture itself. This too should be self-evident.

The Western medicine bag carries Western culture. My African friends would be quick to add that Western medicine is also the theft of the medical arts and sciences from cultures all over the world, stolen from those cultures while the cultures themselves were destroyed. And my African friends are right. In many non-European countries, the Western medicine bag also carries the express vilification of other schools of medical thought, in the same manner that missionaries have vilified much indigenous culture as heresy.

It seems to me it is a good thing when those who carry medicine bags from different cultures learn from each other. But this is not what happens in the missionary world. The medicine practitioners of other cultures are always given not-so-friendly labels like witchdoctor, their practices called witchcraft or sorcery. They are painted as the enemies of the God of the missionary, almost without exception. There is no learning from one another because missionary medicine has taken on the mantle of God; for many native peoples, leaving their traditional approaches and coming to the missionary doctor's hospital is tantamount to kneeling before the missionary's God.

But it is not God, it is Western medicine backed with all the baggage of Western culture. Western medicine has a profound body of knowledge, and I have no objection or say in the matter of whether it sits down with other practices and shares that knowledge. Everyone could benefit from this. But to associate it alongside the message and mission of God is to make it a false gospel. The hope of the world is not, nor can it ever be, in Western medicine.

There is no such thing as Christian medicine. There is only Western medicine (or African or Eastern, among many others). If people of faith want to take their medicine bags when they go into other cultures, that is their business, and it is very possibly a wonderful and compassionate thing to do. But it is not Christian any more than making tents, as Paul did, is Christian. Medicine is not the equivalent of that which Jesus did. Jesus healed without a medicine bag. Missionaries should strive to do the same.

Some have asked if I am saying that missionaries should rely only on miracles as Jesus did, or should they provide medical care at all?

I understand this question, but please bear in mind that I am questioning the role of the missionary as a premise, so I am not going to agree with any answer that begins with "A missionary should ..."

It is the equivalent of asking if Paul should have relied on tentmaking to minister the gospel. He was a tentmaker. He was relying on tentmaking to make a living, perhaps, but there is no suggestion that one who wants to spread the gospel should or should not make tents. If one is a doctor, they should be a doctor. I am only saying that there is no more connection to the skills of Western medicine and the gospel than there is to tentmaking and the gospel.

Right now, while writing this, I am a patient in a Catholic hospital. While in the hospital, I hear prayers for my healing broadcasted at least two times a day. I am not angered or frustrated by this because I understand where I am and why it is this way. The religion of healing is very pervasive. My practitioners are taking good care of me. They are passionate. They are good at the arts of Western and naturopathic medicine. I am grateful. I do not, however, equate their efforts with what the Christ did.

Postscript: Books take a while to put together, and thankfully as of publication, I am in remission. Hopefully, the monster will stay in its cave.

CHAPTER 6

DEVIL'S DEAL

This one is going to get a bit historical. I earned my American and then African history degrees primarily to investigate the subject of this book. Much of what is here comes from my research—a labor that broke my heart.

I want to look, a bit, at two historical figures who directly contributed to the modern missionary and the Golden Age of Missions, Theodore Roosevelt and Charles E. Hurlburt. I am going to make what might seem startling generalizations about these two men. Obviously, few will know Hurlburt, whereas Teddy Roosevelt is famous, at least the sanitized version of him.

Personally, I am no fan of either of these men, but they help explain the dynamic that made the modern missionary world happen.

Roosevelt met with Hurlburt in 1905 (probably not for the first time) at the president's invitation. Both men were public figures who regularly attended high profile functions in New York. Hurlburt was a missionary and in charge of a fledgling missionary organization called the Africa Inland Mission.

These men were on opposite ends of several hotly divided issues in America at the time, but there were two specific issues which separated them. The first was the capacity of what was called the "black race" to be civilized. The second was expansionism in the form of colonial imperialism (the differences between expansionism and colonial imperialism are nuanced and may not be fully addressed here).

THE "BLACK RACE"

Roosevelt was an Ivy League graduate (Harvard and Columbia) well versed in the writings of men like Nathaniel Southgate Shaler, a man who, with his academic credentials, postulated not only the absolute supremacy of the "white races" but also the "innate inability" of blacks to behave morally without the constraints of "white control"—a term used often in the late nineteenth century to justify public lynching as a useful method of control over innate black immorality.

Upon entering public life, Roosevelt said of the so-called black race, "Laziness and shiftlessness, these, and above all, vice and criminality of every kind, are evils more potent for harm to the black race than all acts of oppression of white men together."

(One truth about Roosevelt is he talked a lot, wrote a lot, and never apologized for anything, so quoting him is easy.)

On slavery and against the abolitionist, Roosevelt held a typical Ivy League perspective that slavery was both wrong and, at the same time, necessary for elevating the black race. "The Abolitionists," he said, "have received an immense amount of hysterical praise, which they do not deserve, and have been credited with deeds done by other men, whom they, in reality, hampered and opposed rather than aided."

Charles Hurlburt was, in many ways, the very thing that Roosevelt disdained. Hurlburt's father was an abolitionist activist and lawyer. When Hurlburt was fifteen, his father died in his fight to end slavery. But before he died, he moved his family to Oberlin, Ohio, the hotbed of antislavery activism in America at the time. Charles's education was limited to three years at Oberlin College. This was a school that challenged America's historical pervading view of women and the black race at every turn. It began admitting black students in 1835 (two years after it opened its doors—a scandalous event plastered in papers across the nation) and, in 1837, admitted four women as students, making it the oldest existing coeducational school in America.

In many ways, the movement that began both women's rights and abolitionism in America started at Oberlin College, a small, very conservative school founded in 1833 by two Presbyterian ministers. To attend Oberlin, one had to assert the total, unequivocal equality of both the black race and women. (The rest of America is still trying to catch up today.) Oberlin college professors and students were open participants in John Brown's raid on Harpers Ferry. Harpers Ferry is not a pretty event in history, but the participation of Oberlin faculty and students underscores the radical response to slavery that Charles's father and college cultivated in him. A revolutionary spirit was irrevocably instilled in his intellectual and spiritual DNA.

In contrast to Roosevelt, the "extreme idea" that Hurlburt was raised in was that "the only thing needed for the slave to 'advance' was simply to be free." What Roosevelt and Hurlburt had in common was the idea that a civilized society, as defined by the Western Christian, was necessary and that black people—all over the world—would be best served by abandoning their indigenous social systems and joining more civilized so-called Christian society. The question was not if they, as white men, should try to elevate black people but rather how and when.

COLONIAL IMPERIALISM

Attempting to describe Roosevelt and his quest of American Imperialism is, in my view, so incredible, and perhaps insane, that I fear to lose all credibility in attempting to give details about it. I would urge those who want to find out more for themselves to read a book by Stephen Kinzer, *The True Flag: Theodore Roosevelt, Mark Twain, and the Birth of the American Empire*. It is not the end-all authority on the subject, but it is crisp, cogent, and very professionally researched.

The incredulous quotes of Roosevelt, again, are without end. I am amused at comments made about the current occupant (2020) of the Whitehouse. Most honest historians would agree that crazier men than he have been president, and the craziest of them all, in my view, was Roosevelt. It is with a stunning amount of revisionism that Theodore Roosevelt is considered one of the greatest presidents of American history.

Roosevelt started at least three major conflicts (all under the banner title of the Spanish-American War). These were the result of an open conspiracy of sorts by two, and sometimes three, powerful men who wanted America to join the rest of the civilized world and become a colonial power. Roosevelt was their bully pulpit. When Roosevelt became president, he avoided the international political disaster his conspiracy for colonial dominance created and focused instead on the domestic front.

Roosevelt, despite his distancing himself from further military expansionism, retreated instead to what became known as soft imperialism or neocolonialism.

As an aside, neocolonialism is used differently in modern vernacular where former colonial powers and their puppet states continue oppressive policies and continue the theft of resources from postcolonial states.

Europe had pretty much locked up the world in their own colonial expansionism, but their real power came not from their political conquests but from their so-called moral purpose. The first two expansionist periods in Europe were led by missionaries who focused primarily on education, medicine, and civilization. What became increasingly clear was that these missionaries created dependency everywhere they went.

The soft imperialism strategy went something like this: we can subdue the world, take control of their resources, and make them dependent on our technology by simply sending our missionaries to them. It really didn't matter if the missionary agreed with this purpose. In fact, it was better if they didn't.

The colonial call to missionaries was quite simple: They (soft imperialists) will open the doors to the world for the missionary to go preach whatever brand of the gospel they want. They simply require that, while doing so, the missionary build permanent structures, institutionalize schools, establish medical care, and use Western technology to better the societies they encounter.

I have just described two things, the underlining principle of soft imperialism and the clarion call of every mission society that began in the Golden Age of Missions—roughly 1885–1920. The revised missionary Great Commission: Go into all the world, preaching the gospel, instituting schools, providing medical care, and *appropriate* technology. And lo, the Western world will back you even to the ends of the earth.

And that deal with the colonial devil became, for the missionary world, its altered gospel. To this day, the missionary world has neither the heart nor the character to distance itself from those requirements invested in their foundations. In fact, it wholeheartedly embraces them still.

Colonialism has changed shape and become more subtle, but the spearhead of Western expansionism, by whatever name they are called, is missionaries, and now among them, foreign agencies, religious or not. They are still out there doing the one thing that despot rulers—first colonial powers and later postcolonial rulers—want most from them: creating dependency.

Please read that paragraph again. Please.

Hurlburt had just returned from his first four-year stint in Kenya when he met Roosevelt in New York. He was reviving the African Inland Mission, which was struggling after its founder died just over a year after arriving with a party of six missionaries in what is now Kenya.

There were doors Hurlburt needed to be opened a bit wider. The soft-imperialist president was the best man to do it. Hurlburt needed easier access to Kenya, and Roosevelt paved the way. Later, Hurlburt needed the door to the Congo opened, and he looked to Roosevelt to twist the arm of one of the vilest colonialists in Africa, King Leopold.

I will resist continuing this little history any further. For now, let me mention some of the content of a speech that Roosevelt gave in Kenya when visiting his friend Hurlburt at the founding of a school. At that time, the school included missionary children, Christianized (Westernized) African children, and the children of white settlers: "teach the teachers and train the trainers among the tribes; that you are trying to turn out people who will go back and live among their own ... Turn out leaders who are to take the lead in the uplifting of their own race."

Roosevelt ended the speech with a call that must have warmed the hearts of those early white farmers listening to him: "If you give me a chance in London or anywhere else, I will talk just as straight as I can ... that this is destined to be a white man's [country]." The term "white man's country" was coined by John James Holm (*Holm's Race Assimilation*) to mean "it is the established policy of the white settlers to eventually drive the natives out of the most desirable portion of their own continent and confine them [natives] to the portions in which white men cannot thrive."

It is to this abominable idea of civilization and its progress that missionaries willingly and knowingly have attached themselves. Many of my friends who study the history of missions acknowledge that some early missionaries had a problem with racism.

CHAPTER 7

CULTURE

There are many directions a discussion can go when relating culture and the work of missionaries. Some directions are more obvious or expected than others. I happen to think, however, that some more subtle issues of culture and the missionary are more important than the obvious ones.

What is culture?

Most definitions will loosely describe culture as a collectively regarded set of customs, social institutions, art, a body of knowledge, and historical memory that distinguishes one group of people from another. These definitions may provide good symptomatic descriptions of culture, but they do not get to the heart of culture itself.

On my heavily laden bookshelf at home, I have—among other areas of interest—a large section addressing culture from a variety of philosophical and theological perspectives. All these writings, and my own observations, would seem to agree that the essence of all culture is ideational. In other words, there is a core set of beliefs that make every culture a culture. When a culture is faced with the failure of these core beliefs, it has no choice other than to reinvent itself with a new set of core beliefs. Every other aspect of what is called culture can change and the culture remains intact—but change core beliefs and culture ceases to exist.

The first and most significant response to those core beliefs in a people is language. Language itself is formed around those core beliefs. Language adopts and invents whatever expressions are necessary to adequately encompass those core beliefs for the community. As language develops so do all the other trappings of culture, like the arts, social institutions, historical memory, etc., in response to the core values.

Subcultures that develop within larger cultures do so because they have added one or more additional ideational core beliefs to the primary culture. Often, these subcultures fade and merge back with the primary culture, and occasionally, they become the basis for a new culture.

When I think of culture, I often think of something that a Gikuyu elder used to say to me in my childhood: "Everything contains the seeds of life and death." Indeed, often the very core values that make a culture or subculture strong are the very thing that often will destroy them. The great danger (seed of death) in culture is that the ideational basis must be protected (usually at all costs) for the culture to survive. The ideational basis, or culture, that a person grows up in is usually never questioned very seriously. To do so is almost to self-destruct.

The missionary world, in general, is a subculture within Western culture. In some ways, it could be no other way. Nobody can simply erase their own culture. Nor can one, for the most part, look at their own culture objectively and see both the seeds of life and death that reside in it. One is often inclined to be more forgiving of the failing and faults of their own culture and less forgiving of the failings of another's culture.

Like all cultures and subcultures, the missionary world has its own vocabulary, social institutions, and historical memory. The symptomatic descriptions of the missionary world make it unmistakably a subculture with its own ideational basis. Later, I may try to describe in detail what I see as its ideational basis.

Please understand that I am serious when I say that I do not blame the honest intentions or good character of many, if not most, of the missionaries that I grew up with in Africa. What I question is the Western subculture called the "missionary" and the ideational basis that allows it to exist at all. Particularly good people, who accept as normative an aberrant ideational basis, can cause disasters in the name of kindness and love.

That last paragraph was the entire reason I am writing this chapter. If you would be so kind as to give it due consideration, I would deeply appreciate it.

I remember as a child having an emotional conflict as I watched the missionary world around me. I saw, with the support of churches and nonprofit organizations, buildings built, roads constructed, dams raised to produce electricity, hospitals erected, schools—the list is endless. On one hand, I admired the courage and ingenuity of the people I grew up with, but on the other hand, I had this nagging struggle in the back of my mind. I could see no correlation between what was happening and the teachings and example of the Christ Himself. The justifications came instead, from cherry-picked verses rather than the teachings, examples, and guiding principles of the Teacher and Lord that all professed to follow. It seemed (and seems) to me that the actual teaching and example of the Christ is the exact opposite of the missionary world. How can an entire enterprise of believers be so confident and courageous and yet not be as conflicted, as I was, about their basis for doing what they were doing?

These questions have never left me. They have driven me to study history and to read every missionary book I could get my hands on. In the process, I began to study culture. My reason for studying culture was to look at the effect of cross-culture communication, as I was always certain that the missionary world was terrible at communication with other cultures. Indeed, I still think that, but the aha moment of my readings on culture was the realization that the reason very good people do and continue to do very destructive things has little to do with their intentions and everything to do with the ideational basis of their culture. In this case, the missionary culture.

What I have already suggested, and will continue to point out, is the ideational basis of the missionary is the product of soft colonialism not the teachings of the Christ. While missionaries have long since separated themselves from their colonial past in terms of rhetoric, they have yet to separate themselves from their own ideational basis. The problem is if they repudiate their own ideational basis, they will cease to exist.

My answer to this quandary is simple: go home.

In my last decade or so of life, I have spent many hours listening to elderly Gikuyu men and women, the very people I grew up with as a son of missionaries. I approached these interviews not as a believer, which I am, not as one seeking to help them in any way. I listened to try to learn who they are from their own point of view.

The results of these interviews have been many, not the least of which is a deep admiration I have gained for who these people are and an astonishment at how far removed their reality is from the perception of those from within the missionary world.

Most importantly, what I came to understand, in a small way, is just how fundamentally damaging the missionary world was and is to them, how deeply they were and are misunderstood, how deep and resentful the anger is in many. It was and has been for me a very painful journey.

My most painful realization was that a message of "peace on earth, goodwill toward men" has been turned into a message of chaos, destruction, disenfranchisement, racism, and perpetual suppression.

The response I get from my missionary friends is, "Yes, we made some mistakes in the past, but the gospel was shared, and we have seen that God has blessed that."

Some mistakes? This is the gospel?

CHAPTER 8

BABEL

I want to try to address the idea and issues of language and culture as it relates to missions and missionaries in a different way. In doing so, I am reminded of a comment in the movie *The Gods Must Be Crazy*: "I know the words, but I don't understand the meaning." Actually, this is a misquote, but it gets at the general idea.

I have long understood that I see the world in different terms than most of the people that I have known, including my own family and friends. At various times in my life, this difference has been all the proof I needed to validate my own version of stupid, and at other times, a modicum of intelligence. All of this makes me about normal, I suppose.

All too often in my experience, however, I find myself at odds with others on a variety of issues. What seems obviously true to many seems patently false or grievously wrong to me. Sometimes, like in *The Gods Must Be Crazy*, I feel like I am using the same words as everyone else, but at the same time, it is as if I am speaking a different language. In short, much of what has often been considered conventional wisdom is erroneous to me or, perhaps, confusing, as summed up in the word "babel."

Besides being terribly self-indulging, the last paragraph describes something that people who have been raised in a culture that is foreign to their parents' culture often have in common. We are sometimes called third-culture kids (TCKs) because we live in a world caught between two very divergent cultural ideations. As a result, words often take on variations in meaning in our minds that conflict with both the world we grew up in and the culture of our parents. I mention this as an illustration of the following.

A TALE ABOUT THE TALE OF THE TOWER OF BABEL

This tale may or may not reflect any similarity of the intended purpose and message of the story of the Tower of Babel as told in the Hebrew scriptures.

Remember, if you will, the basic definition of culture that I developed in the previous chapter—that culture is fundamentally ideational (based on a set of beliefs) from which all other aspects develop. The very first act of those beliefs is language. Core beliefs always develop new or modified words that are uniquely suited to describe and develop ideas around that ideational basis.

One day in the murky past, some folk were working on their very own ziggurat. This structure, a tall man-made tower built to the heavens, was, perhaps, the first of its kind ever built. It was constructed by a people united in their theology, united in their language, and united in their common practice.

The Creator of all Things, as the story goes, took exception to the ziggurat. The tower built to the heavens, it turns out, was a shift away from the Creator's instructions for mankind to spread out over the earth. The tower represented the human's desire to be fruitful and remain rather than to be fruitful and spread out. Humans, taking exception to the Creator's intentions, developed instead a theology of entrenchment and empowerment. "Otherwise we will be scattered over the face of the earth." Clearly, an ideational core had been developed and was expressed first by language and then by a tower built of brick and tar.

The problem, as the Creator saw it, was that all humans spoke the same language—a language that had developed from an ideational core that found expression in the language "let us" and resulted in unified cultural action, building a tower intended to resist the Creator's call to spread out.

The solution the Creator came up with was brilliant. It may have been ten or twelve—no, I think it was likely seven messengers. Each messenger took up a position in a different area of the massive tower project. Each messenger had been given a different aspect of the Creator's nature to discuss as they worked shoulder to shoulder with their fellow workers. As each brick was laid so was the seed of an idea. Each messenger inspired a different idea in the mind of the workers around them. The workers talked about these ideas among themselves when they took breaks and at home at the end of each long day. Seven quite different aspects of the nature of the Creator were discussed, each in isolation to the other.

What happens when within a majority culture a new seed or ideation is added to the core ideations that make up the culture? Well first, a subculture develops. Along with subculture comes new vocabulary and modifications of meaning on existing vocabulary—the beginning of a new language.

When seven subcultures began to adopt new words and redefine old words, can you imagine the confusion (babel)?

Soon seven new ziggurats were being constructed, and the original project stopped for the lack of a sufficient workforce—the march to fill the earth had begun again.

Language does not beget new language, but rather, the introduction of new ideation creates language. From a tiny piece of the

Creator's eternity in their hearts, each culture develops their own language and practices that make them unique to all other cultures.

You may challenge my understanding of what the Tower of Babel story was all about. I am not concerned if you see the story as real or myth or spiritual myth. I am using my perspective of the story to make a point about language and culture—and how the missionary model has misunderstood the basis of the message of the gospel—and, along with it, the basis of its own culture.

Too many years ago, I first started thinking about and reading about culture. One book that I came to love dearly was *Culture and Biblical Hermeneutics*. It was written by William J. Larkin Jr. I once attended a lecture Larkin gave at a theological conference, and it was like a bolt of lightning in my puny brain.

Over the years since, I have grown to appreciate his understanding of culture, but at the same time, I have come to disagree with one of his primary conclusions. You see, for him, all the ideational bases of culture are in rebellion to God. They are man's attempt to create God in their own image. The gospel then, in his view, is the antidote for that rebellion. While I think his analysis of what culture is remains a huge influence in my life, I take some exception to his idea of the purpose and role of Biblical hermeneutics in culture.

Why was Paul "determined to know nothing among them other than Christ and Him Crucified?" Why did the Christ himself say, "If you have seen me, you have seen the Father?" The message of the gospel is not about establishing a new religion or education or holding fear, especially the fear of hell over the heads of the heathen.

The gospel reestablishes the ideational bases which informs all cultures and brings them back through their own ideational process to God. The gospel is not interested in modernity, nor English, nor Western education, nor medicine, nor foreign aid, and, if you will allow me to say it, not even the religion of Christianity—these are all elements of a false gospel.

When Jewish believers separated themselves from Gentile believers as described in the book of Galatians or through the act of circumcision as described in the book of Acts, thereby attempting to force Gentile believers to follow Jewish customs, Paul called this a false gospel and "accursed." It may be understandable, considering the times, why the Judaizers wanted to get the Gentiles to follow their customs, but if so doing was condemned as a false gospel, how much more so introducing Western civilization as part and parcel to the gospel?

Many followers of Christ simply do not believe that a message of love and reconciliation is enough without the trinkets of their own external culture. In fact, the so-called gospel that Africa knows is largely a religion of exclusion, hell, distinction, and submission without recourse. In what possible way does this reflect peace on earth, good will to men?

Religious buildings, pastors, denominations, worship services, ministries, missions, revivals, the list goes on and on of things that have developed in Western Christianity that do not have their origins in the scriptures, especially in the teachings of Jesus. Many of these things have their origins, instead, in Western paganism. So, let me get this straight, we can introduce elements of Western paganism into our missionary message, but we condemn those whose practices we determine to be pagan?

Hypocrisy, no less than Peter's.

If one can justify worshiping in a man-made structure, facing passively a man you call pastor, or having a gathering for worship that you call "going to church"—then such a person can say nothing about another who desires to worship God under a Mugumo tree or face a mountain that represents to them the holiness of the Creator God or waiting on a man to return from communion with God to deliver a message from the Creator of All Things. All come from outside of any teaching of the Christ.

If one set of actions is unacceptable and pagan, then so is the other. If one set of actions is acceptable and Christian, then so is the other.

The message of the Christ has no baggage, does not stay where it is not welcome, and does not stay long even where it is welcome. Ours is an ideational campaign. It is not a confrontation to change the physical compositions of cultures.

CHAPTER 9

CHILDREN

One of the more startling differences between the mission and method of the Christ and the mission and method of modern missionaries is children.

It is easy and simple to describe the relationship of the Christ and children. When the children were brought to the Christ for Him to put His hands on them and to pray for them, the Christ allowed it and rebuked those who tried to stop the young ones from being brought to Him. It is key to notice that they were brought to Him—it was they or their loved ones who took the initiative, not the Christ. Beyond this, the Christ encouraged childlike faith and humility—children as metaphors, not targets. The child conversions in the scriptures are limited to household conversions.

The separation of children from their families for the purpose of conversion, education, or change in behavior was never in view. Never.

The Christ was focused on the poor, sick, needy, tax collectors, prostitutes, townsfolk, soldiers, and deeply religious. The method was always direct and never easy. It was never directed specifically toward children, and there never was an attempt to separate children from their parents to take advantage of their more impressionable minds. Never.

The relationship between modern missionaries and children can't possibly be described in two simple paragraphs. In fact, it might take several books to unpack the complicated and (in my view) convoluted methods devised by missionaries toward children.

Separating children from their parents for indoctrination and enlightenment is not a novel concept in the Western world, but it seems to me, it is a cowardly one. It is a tacit admission that the message itself is too weak to withstand the objections of a mature mind. This, I think, is the real issue. The modern gospel is so weak, so unacceptable, so insulting to intelligence that it must first be engrained in young, malleable minds to have any chance of lasting through the years in a mature mind.

The strength of the message always informs the method.

Jesus was the friend of the most unlovable people possible, the very demographics that modern "child evangelism" avoids in search of more impressionable candidates. Christ loved the unlovable; missionaries and evangelists focus too often on the most lovable—the children of the unlovable. It seems that everyone sees the moral outrage of child evangelism except for the evangelists themselves.

There was a recent chat on Facebook with two amazingly brilliant Kenyan thinkers. One posted a bit on a conversation he had with a "First Nation citizen of Australia." In it, he describes the unspeakable evil of the "Black Act" laws that lasted into the early 1980s. Included was children's forced separation from their parents to be educated and trained to be domestic workers and laborers by—guess who?—missionaries.

By these laws, children were literally animals legally hunted down and killed. Animals. Trophies. And intimately connected to missionaries.

The other Kenyan contributed similar stories to the Australian one, from Canada. Churches involved directly in a "legacy" of "utter destruction" of a people and their culture all in the name of the "Good News."

There are so many things to talk about when it comes to missionaries and children. I really need to address them separately and, in more detail, because they are all too big and too important and the gateway to the destruction for which missionaries are the most culpable. Not only toward the third world, but toward their own children.

For now, let me say this. The evangelization of children is pure cowardice.

What did Jesus do?

Christ was the friend of the prostitutes, the drunkards, the tax collectors, the general worst of the worst riffraff of society. He was their friend—they, if anybody, were His mission. On second thought, no, it wasn't them; it seems His disciples were his mission, not just the riffraff or the sick, but that is another topic. He was also the friend of the religious, but He didn't give the religious much slack.

I suspect He was the friend of the riffraff because, generally, they are the truly honest people in society. For the master, that must have been refreshing. It is for me.

Christ did not evangelize children. When the parents of children brought them to Jesus, He only said, "Let them come."

CHAPTER 10

BOARDING SCHOOL EVANGELISM

One of the things that astonishes me the most is the cognitive dissonance that occurs between missionaries and boarding schools. Boarding schools have a less than distinguished history. There are cases of boarding-type schools that go back as far as the Spartans of Greek lore, and probably much further back than that.

In terms of the more modern idea of missionary boarding schools, the beginning seems to go back to British colonialism in India in the early sixteen hundreds where the focus was directly and unapologetically on the "Westernization and indoctrination of future leaders."

Boarding schools were born in racism and assumptions of cultural superiority. The concept spread around the colonial world like wildfire. For the colonies, it was an effective way of subduing; for the missionary, it was the educational vehicle for the central sacred cow of their faith—the Bible.

Of course in American history, the story of missionaries and Native American schools is known well enough, along with the devastating effects it had on both indigenous communities and children—young children no longer quite able to fit back into their own culture but still separated by racial prejudice from fitting fully into the dominant culture.

At the spearhead of it all were the religious nuances of the missionaries.

As elsewhere, the American government paid missionaries to educate and later to provide "off-reservation" boarding schools to "better assimilate" native children. This was a terrible disaster, the ramifications of which are still felt today in Native American cultures. Please provide the Christian principle that gives impetus for believers to participate with governments that force children to be separated from their parents and then teach obedience to those governments.

Why are Christians forever in bed with the agenda of the mighty (principalities and powers) rather than defending against the injustices visited upon the disenfranchised?

I grew up in a place called Kijabe in Kenya. As was typical of the early missionary movement, the first missionaries at Kijabe established a boarding school for young Gikuyu girls. From the perspective of a letter written by one of the missionaries, a headmistress, to her supporters in America, a "wonderful thing" was happening at Kijabe. Young girls were being taken from their parents and hidden to rescue them from the wicked and ungodly practices of the Agikuyu. If it was too late for their parents, perhaps these young girls could be salvaged from damnation.

The missionaries disguised the girls so that when their parents came looking for them, they couldn't be recognized. God was to be glorified for hiding these young girls in "plain sight" of their parents.

The text cruelly used in the justification of this practice came from the King James Version of the words of Jesus in the book of Matthew: "Suffer the little children to come unto Me and forbid them not." If you are not familiar with old English, the meaning of "suffer" used to include the concept of "allow." It simply says, let the children come, don't stop them.

The "allow" instruction was directed to the disciples of Christ, who did not want the snot-nosed brats to get so close—the Master, after all, had more important people to talk to. The instructions were not to the children's parents. It would be appalling if what was being implied was, as the missionary letter implies, that children should be taken against their parents' wishes and hidden "in plain sight" so that their ungodly parents would never see them again—all in the name of what? The gospel?

THE PATTERN

In the missionary world, all too often the idea of "suffer the children" includes—without a doubt—suffering, in the most common use of the term. This practice is and always was evil.

The practice of removing children from their parents, believe it or not, is mysteriously missing from the pages of Christian writings—except when used in service to colonialism and other principalities and powers.

The example I gave at Kijabe, is tame. This practice—among others—which focused on separating children from parents, happened all over Kenya, across all missionary agencies. It was, in part, a litmus test by the colonial powers for opening new opportunities for mission societies to expand into new areas of work.

I am not familiar enough with the first colonial movement (400–1000ish AD) to know their practices, but the more recent two colonial expansion periods used this practice of child separation as a regular feature, and it was by far the most effective way to dull the senses and destroy the culture of any people. It happened everywhere. Literally.

71

The forced reeducation of Native Americans is not as far back in the distant historical past as one might imagine. The reeducation program in Alaska, especially of the Aleuts, is within the lifetime of people today. That is an unimaginable saga. One redeeming tale is the example of the Eastern Orthodox church, which in my view, literally rescued the entire population of Aleuts from certain death after the despicable acts against them by the US government in World War II.

Many Native Americans will say reeducation is still actively going on today.

CHAPTER 11

CALLING

Those of you who are in opposition to missionaries might want to pay a bit of attention. This is, in my view, the single most motivating reason why missionaries do what they do, no matter how crazy it may seem.

I want to address the idea of the Christian "calling," especially the calling to be a missionary. A calling is the basis, in the minds of many missionaries and mission societies, for the legitimization of their endeavors. I think most in the missionary world will recognize that what I just wrote is true.

The ultimate defense for amazingly questionable behavior (sending your children off to boarding school so you can better serve God, for example) is an appeal to one's calling. Many are the stories of missionary kids who endured years of abuse at schools and elsewhere, who were threatened into silence, because speaking out would derail their parents' calling and work for God.

There are some good books on this subject, which I may address at another time.

However, if I can, I am going to make my case here without direct argument. Instead, I want to tell just a bit of my story—the story of my calling to, presumably, go back to Africa. If I were to tell this whole story, it would take pages, perhaps another book. So, I will try to be as succinct as possible.

My personal questioning of the justification for the missionary began as a young child of missionaries. Though the questions have become more complicated, throughout my life, the conviction that the entire missionary scheme is built on error has never left me. I must admit that in those early days, the idea that missionaries had a personal calling from God tripped me up just a tad—I had no good answer for this back then.

In telling a bit about my story, I am taking a great risk. Those of you who do not believe in such things may think less of me for what I am claiming to be true about my experiences. Those of you who do believe in such a calling may think less of me because of my ultimate response—or lack thereof.

It was on my thirtieth birthday when I began to receive my calling to go back to Africa.

I happened, in those days, to own a small trucking company, North Georgia Freight Service. On my birthday, I was making a delivery to Shaw Industries (as I remember it), a carpet factory in Dalton, Georgia. As I was waiting to have the freight signed in, I stood next to a gentleman with a strong East African accent. Mind you, this was in the 1980s in north Georgia, and I had never met an African up to that time in that area. I took a chance and greeted the man in Swahili. A big smile crossed his face, and I had a sweet conversation with a man my age who was born in Kenya near where I grew up. He was, as I remember, selecting carpet samples to send back to a broker in Kenya. It was a happy happenstance, and I would have just filed it into my memory banks as such, until the next day.

The next day, I was in Lafayette (I think it was), Georgia, making a delivery to a construction project. It was there while having lunch in a small diner, I heard the family behind me speaking in Swahili.

Lafayette, Georgia, in the eighties—really? I introduced myself and had a wonderful conversation with a Kenyan family. I left wondering at the statistical odds of such meetings happening twice in two days. Again, I still might have filed this neatly into the memory bank of happenstance, except it happened again every day for seven days in a row. I was getting just a bit freaked out. But before I go on, let me tell you about the last of the seven days.

On the seventh day, I was making a delivery at a small hotel in Calhoun, Georgia. The young men who came out to sign for the delivery spoke with heavy Indian accents. They signed the name Patel. This has got to be as common a name, if not more so, in India as Smith is reported to be in the United States. But I made a comment that I knew a man named Patel in Kenya who I had admired. Describing the man, I told them that he had left Kenya to go to some unknown country a couple of years before I left for the United States. As I told my story, one of the men excused himself and returned a few minutes later with the very Patel that I had known as a child in Kenya.

I hope you will understand when I say that this was one of the most bizarre weeks of my life. A direct conversation with an angel, however, would have made it a bit easier to understand what purpose, if any, was behind all these encounters.

That day, I called a good friend of mine, John Stringer, and told him that I needed to go fishing with him. I needed his take on the week that I had just had. I must have sounded a bit freaked out because John dropped everything, and we went fishing all night on Chickamauga Lake, close to Chattanooga, Tennessee. After I gave him my story, his advice was: this was likely a God thing; it clearly had to do with Kenya; I should start praying and seeking counsel from spiritual people, ASAP.

I knew this was good advice, but frankly, my experience was starting to sound a lot like one of the many missionary calling stories I had heard growing up. I had long since written off missionary work, as I considered it was based on principles contrary to the teachings of the Christ.

I felt faced with a much gentler version of Abraham being asked to sacrifice his son on an altar to God. Was I willing to become that which I believed was contrary to the will of God if I felt God was the one who asked me to do it? And, so far however, I had not heard the word missionary, so perhaps I was safe.

I spent the next seven days praying and seeking counsel. Every day I prayed, and every day I got an answer so bizarre that I fear even the most open-minded of you would not believe me.

However, let me share the last answer to my prayers that I received. At the end of the second seven days, my head filled with advice—full of loving contradictions—and strange answers to prayer, it occurred to me that there was a theologian I knew in Wisconsin, Jon Zens, whom I admired and whom I would love to hear from on the subject. So, in prayer while driving home, I asked if I should somehow go to Wisconsin and spend some time with Jon.

I had another friend, Mike Miller, who had left Georgia and was, as I recall, living in Boston.

(If you are not up on your geography, you might look up and see the distances between Massachusetts, Georgia, and Wisconsin.)

Shortly after I got home, I got a call from Mike. He said he was on his way to Georgia to pick me up and take me to Wisconsin. He had an unshakable feeling that he was supposed to take me up to see Jon for a few days. He planned to pick me up the next morning, so I needed to get ready fast. I did, and a couple days later, I was in Wisconsin.

Mike had been well on his way before I prayed about going to see Jon Zens.

Just pretend for a moment you had experienced two weeks like this. I imagine that you too would be convinced that something was happening that was far beyond your rational capacity to explain.

At this point, I must begin skipping a bit through the story.

If you recognize the phrase "cloud by day, fire by night," perhaps you will understand what I mean when I say I was *led* by these events, and others of their type, to sell my business, pack up my family, and move to Washington State to join a Christian "tentmaking" mission group.

Everything we owned that I could not fit in our Suburban and homemade trailer was sold or given away, and we drove across the country.

I was a bit worried that my overloaded truck and trailer were going to be hard on my brakes, so I brought along an extra set of brake shoes and kept handy the tools I would need to change them just in case. I am not a mechanic, but I could do that much back then.

True enough, coming down a steep hill near Yellowstone National Park, my brakes failed, and I precariously, but safely, got to the bottom of the grade and pulled off the road. I got out my tools, brake shoes, and jack and began to get ready to replace the worn brakes on the side of the road. Soon I learned that the truck was different than the models that I had worked on before, and this one required a large Allen wrench. I had no Allen wrenches.

Frustrated, I decided to jack up the tire anyway and see if there were any other tools I still needed. As I jacked, I think I was getting myself ready to flag down the next passing cowboy and see if they could take me to purchase the tools in some nearby town. Then, as the tire lifted, I noticed a piece of metal on the ground under where the tire had been sitting. It was an Allen wrench—the size I needed. It was the only additional tool I needed to change the brakes, and it was resting under my tire at the exact place my truck has stopped. Cloud by day, fire by night.

On the day I arrived in the Seattle area, all the extraordinary happenings disappeared. And my life slowly began to fall apart.

The Christian tentmaking organization dissolved within six months of my arrival. I was in complete confusion. My abilities as an entrepreneur and businessman were met with failure after failure, and my already strained marriage was quickly disintegrating. I had sold my business and burnt all my bridges. The heavens were as brass, my prayers and tears unheeded. I came to understand a little bit of what it means to be forsaken by God.

This is when we met the Testermans. I think his name was Jeff; I don't remember his wife's name. They were the most unusual family I have ever met in my life. I am still not certain if their DNA was human or angel. We met them twice. The first time we met, I felt a compelling need to sit down and talk with them. The second time, I told them my story in far more detail than I am telling now. I asked Jeff what he thought I should do.

Guidance from an angel proved to be a bit easier to understand.

Jeff gave what was, for myself at the time, the most revolutionary answer. I knew as soon as he opened his mouth that he was correct. He told me that I should not do anything about my experiences or calling. Do absolutely nothing.

Personally, I am an intuitive leaper, and I usually don't need too many details to put something together. Jeff could have stopped there, because scales dropped off my eyes, and I could see that he was right and that it was illustrated in story after story in the Christian and Hebrew writings and teachings. The only legitimate response to a calling was to do nothing. Absolutely nothing. If it is of God, it will happen; if not, it won't. Not my problem.

How had I missed it for so many years—my blindness toward my life in a missionary culture where a calling was the basis for one's right and obligation "to go" and "to do" the work of God. Suddenly I understood that doing something was the poisoned chalice—or perhaps the forbidden fruit—for someone who feels called. The so-called Great Commission, which is the proof-text for almost every evangelical mission endeavor, has absolutely nothing to do with this subject. The One who spoke those words is the epitome of doing nothing. From the Gospel of John: "I can do nothing of my own accord."

Jeff and his family left heading for Tennessee the next day.

My life went to hell.

A couple of years later, I was in a crippling depression that lasted about fourteen years. During this time, I lost my marriage, was unable to be a meaningful father to my sons, lost my health, and went bankrupt. I was told by my doctor that if I continued down the path I was on physically, I had less than five years to live. That seemed much too long at the time.

Well-meaning friends suggested that my troubles were because I had refused God's calling. Other well-meaning friends told me that I was being faithful to God's calling and this was my "time of testing in the wilderness" (I liked and hated this explanation).

As part of my climb out of the depression, I decided to do two things: First, I began to study African History—I have always been a hobby historian, but more importantly, I thought it would clarify a bit more about myself and my past. I grew up in the context of Africa, I think differently than anyone I know, and I wanted to understand if this came from my Kenyan youth, living among the Agikuyu people. Second, I studied creative writing—I had always wanted to write a critique of the mission field and the culture that surrounds it, but my writing skills sort of sucked.

I beat my depression, in part, by getting my undergraduate and graduate degrees in creative writing, American history, and, later, African history. My master's degree fieldwork was in Kenya, interviewing elderly Gikuyu men and women, learning about their culture and past from their point of view rather than through the tinted lens of my missionary childhood.

Something odd happened in the process. I am more connected now to Africa than I ever was before. I am more connected to Kenya now than I have ever been. I am deeply in love with my Kenyan friends and admire greatly the culture, educational system, historical beliefs (theology), and system of justice of the pre-Agikuyu.

I am especially connected to those Kenyans (not just Gikuyu) who call themselves the Errant Natives, who see so much more clearly the duplicity and problems with the missionary world than I see now or saw years ago as a child. They have taught me to understand so much more about the dark underbelly of the colonial and missionary beast. They are still my teachers, and I am forever grateful to them for helping me to remove the last of a fundamental blindness that I did not know I had.

Ironically, in their antagonism against my faith, they have caused my faith to grow deeper. They minister to me much more than I could ever minister to them.

All this, and I do not live in Africa. I live in Washington state. Is this what my calling was about all along? Perhaps my calling was to write this book. Or just to post annoying missives on Facebook. I don't know, and I don't care. My calling is not in my hands, and it is not my problem. It never was.

So many scales lifted over the years.

I mentioned earlier that I began an outline of a book I wanted to write about missionaries in my early twenties. In my midthirties, after significant theological shifts, I revised the outline. In my forties I tried to write a few chapters. My fifties were spent in depression, so not much happened. Now, I am writing again with a different title and a radically different perspective. I find nothing in those early outlines that I really agree with anymore. I am glad that book never made it past my files.

I am now married to the world's most perfect woman. I am at peace. And for the first time in my life, there is fundamental happiness—even amid a touch of life-threatening disease and a modest bit of suffering.

If one can recall the Hebrew stories of Joseph, Moses, and David, one can see the importance of doing nothing. David, in fact, seemed to go further than any other character. When he was anointed to be King, he returned to the field and remained a shepherd. Twice when he had the life of his predecessor king in his hands—literally a sword to his throat—he refused to take what had been promised him with his own hands. Even if one has had the chance to study the chronology of Paul in the epistles, one can see that it was years after his encounter with the Christ before others, "through the Holy Spirit," saw fit to send him to do the work that very possibly had been burning in his heart since that encounter on the road to Damascus. These are the obvious examples of callings in which the recipient chose not to act. There are many more.

The most important thing I have learned about my calling is that the best response is to do nothing.

CHAPTER 12

KNOWING THE ENEMY

It seems to me that one of the most important elements in a conflict is to properly identify the enemy. It is way too easy to blame those on the forefront of actions taken instead of what was behind those actions. In the early days, the various cultures in Kenya understood that the colonial power that was dominating them was not, as they said, "the head of the snake." The head rather was in England. That was the source of the power, and that was the real enemy to their way of life.

The problem with identifying the wrong enemy is that it becomes very confusing. There were colonial leaders in Kenya that worked against the colonial intentions and tried tirelessly to preserve or get land returned to the original owners.

There was one land commissioner in Nairobi who threatened to put some missionary in legal jeopardy and expel them because they did a "taking" on a piece of land that they thought would benefit the mission work. In a letter to the missionary, the commissioner said (not a direct quote): "We are stealing their land, we are taking away their livelihood. How can you justify taking more in the name of God?" The fact is, there are several areas in Kenya that are still in the hands of the original owners because of acts like this colonial land commissioner.

During the so-called Mau Mau period in Kenya, large numbers of Gikuyu men and women were rounded up and accused of being Mau Mau. They were detained, tortured, and then frequently hanged, or shot. One common practice, especially if the British soldiers were certain they had a lorry full of actual fighters, was to stop in the forests on the way to a prison camp. They would let the prisoners out and tell them that it was their lucky day and they were letting them go. As the Gikuyu men and women fled into the surrounding woods, the British soldiers and their loyalist allies would shoot the fugitives in the back. They would then drag the bodies to their commanders and claim that the rebels had tried to escape. There is one British commander, well known to surviving Mau Mau fighters, who, when he got wind that this was going to happen, would go to the Gikuyu on the lorry and tell them: "When the lorry stops, don't run. They won't shoot you unless you run. If you do run, you are dead." Some former fighters, now elders, I talked to claim this one British commander saved hundreds or, perhaps, thousands of lives.

In one very real way, both the land commissioner and the British commander were the enemy. It is inescapable that they were, after all, part and parcel of an invasion that destroyed lives and cultures. It is also fair, I think, that in the context in which these two men found themselves, they were not monsters; they were among the noble of humanity. It is a difficult juxtaposition.

However, calling these two men the enemy would misidentify the true enemy, and fighting them as individuals would never win the war. They were not the head of the snake.

I grew up with missionaries. Among my heroes and ideas of what composes the best of humanity are individual missionaries. I have seen missionaries give their lives very willingly to protect the lives of the Africans around them. I have seen beautiful people give up their fortune to live in circumstances that destroyed their bodies because of the deep love and care they had for Africans. This was not just about a salvation show—it was humanity broken over the wrongs that were done to other humans and being willing to give up their lives to see it end.

Of course, I have seen the very worst in missionaries too. I have seen abuse, sexual deviancy, unbelievable racism, cultural superiority, and willing abetting of the colonial scheme.

Ultimately, my point is this. Missionaries, in my view, are not the enemy. They are, instead, unwitting foot soldiers for the enemy. I don't think that most missionaries understand this.

It will take the entire book, I think, to persuade a very few toward an understanding of what the real enemy is, even though I have mentioned this enemy in every chapter so far.

The Western world is very apt at historical amnesia. Western missionaries, like the culture that bred them, prefer to disassociate themselves from the past—"We're not like that anymore." But in so doing, they continue the exact patterns of foot soldiers for the very past that they now eschew.

I do not question motivations. I do not question intent. I do not claim insight into the minds of others. I am not so wise or skilled. I simply look at patterns and their consequences.

CHAPTER 13

CHIEFS AND
MISSIONARIES

I am going to try to do the impossible and distill volumes of information into a few short paragraphs.

The Agikuyu, like many others in East Africa, did not have a chief or chiefdom system of governance before colonialism. They had thrown off their chief system a couple hundred years before colonialism when a man, loosely translated to "King Gikuyu," ruled the Gikuyu in a tyrannical way—this king is not the same as the original Gikuyu father.

If you know anything about the historical period after the Cromwell revolution in England, perhaps you are aware of a debate that lasted almost a century subsequently. The question at hand was what, in fact, was the perfect form of government—anything but a king. Those debates resulted (for better or worse) in the American and French revolutions.

In a similar way, ruling agemates among the Gikuyu, after disposing of their tyrannical king, debated a better system of government— because they also wanted something other than a king.

What that generation of Gikuyu thinkers came up with was a combination of independent self-rule of each household, community, and clan along with a multilayered system of elder counsels who provided judicial oversight, operating at various levels throughout the culture. There was no need in their system for a legislative or executive or judicial branch. Lawsuits, disputes, and questions of procedure were brought to the appropriate elder counsel. A system of appeals was in place until, if necessary, it was brought to the ultimate elder counsel—the closest comparison would be America's Supreme Court.

Along with these levels of judicial oversight, the Gikuyu put in place a system of ritual, agemate alliances, storytelling, marriage, and teachers (*gichandi*), which kept the entire community together.

THE OGRE, THE HYENA, AND THE RABBIT (OR SQUIRREL)

Among the repertoire of almost every Bantu culture is a set of similar folktales based on three characters, the ogre, the hyena, and the rabbit or squirrel. In precolonial Agikuyu folklore, the third character was a type of squirrel, but with Swahili (also a Bantu culture) becoming the lingua franca of East Africa, the Gikuyu generally adopted the Swahili use of a rabbit.

The stories that surrounded these three characters gave storytellers the basis for more than just entertainment. The three characters were designed to show the three characteristics of being human that could threaten the cohesive nature of a communal society.

The squirrel is the least harmful. This is the jokester, the one that laughs and takes delight in the well-placed prank that humiliates or embarrasses another. Most often, the laugh is played on the hyena or the ogre. But nevertheless, the one who does not take the community seriously and laughs at the expense of others can never be taken seriously. Their voice is not heard in the council of elders. They may be entertaining, but they do nothing to create unity in the culture.

The hyena is a person driven by insatiable appetite and greed, and their concern is not the cohesiveness of the people. It is always best to recognize the hyena and protect the community from their selfish ambition. They are never to be trusted, and they are never to be allowed to sit in the council of elders.

The ogre is one who appears to be a part of the culture (in our case the Gikuyu culture), but in fact, they are out to eat or devour the culture. The culture and its members are the prey. Ogres hide their features and dress and look Gikuyu. Their words are slick and enticing, and they will lead a person, a homestead, or a clan into their trap and then hold them captive as they feed on their victims.

If you are Gikuyu, you are no doubt grimacing at this cursory summary. Please forgive me. But what I want to point out is that the Agikuyu did not have chiefs, and they put in place a system of checks, songs, and stories designed to prevent the tyranny of a king or chief from ever happening again. This may surprise some of the younger members of that culture, who may have assumed that chiefs were always a part of their history.

The ogre-hyena-rabbit stories were used to insulate the Gikuyu from the types of characters that might return them to a tyrannical rule that they had disposed of for at least two centuries.

COLONIALISM

When the colonialists invaded the Gikuyu lands, they had a problem. There was no head to the Gikuyu snake for them to cut off. From the Western world's perspective, there must be a leader, even if such a one is not called a king. The Gikuyu system of cultural adhesiveness and elder judiciary made any type of top-to-bottom administration unnecessary. The Gikuyu, as well as other East African cultures, had singular figures that rose throughout their history, especially in times of crises or war, but these men were not executors, legislators, or the judiciary. They rose responding to a need and then went home to their farmlands.

But colonialism already had a solution to this problem, as it was not the first time in colonial expansion that they had encountered it. The solution: establish chiefs and negotiate only with them. This same pattern occurred in much of North America. Precolonial Native Americans, for the most part, did not have chiefs either—at least in the Western concept of the word. Certainly, they had big men who rose to the occasion in a crisis, but chiefdom was not part of the administrative mechanism of most of their cultures.

THE MISSIONARY

How do you establish chiefs in a chief-less society, one might ask? Well, here is how it was done.

Missionaries in each "ward" were assigned as the representatives of the Gikuyu people in their area.

Imagine the audacity of this. Western born and bred, limited language skills at best, living in fortress compounds, armed with the presupposition of Western superiority, and with no background in the culture beyond a few works by Western anthropologists—how did this qualify missionaries to be the representatives of a people that became the chattel of colonialism?

The ultimate assignment or responsibility for a missionary was to find strong leaders among the Gikuyu to appoint as chiefs in the various wards.

Praise God, the missionary responds. As we win souls to Christ, we will identify those with strong leadership skills to be the chiefs of these people, and they will ultimately lead the culture to Christ.

I am going to brush past the racism and cultural bigotry of this concept. I am going to brush past the idea that missionaries were in such cahoots with the colonial scheme that they dared agree to the role given to them. I will address in some other essay, perhaps, how utterly this mission fails in the most fundamental aspects of the leadership, as defined by the Christ, that the missionary claims to follow.

Instead, I want to mention the devastation this scheme caused to the Gikuyu culture and, in my view, continues to cause today.

For the West, the marks of leadership that are most sought after are the very same marks identified in Gikuyu culture as those of the hyena and the ogre, those of a character that will destroy a people if such persons come into power. For the man who is willing to sacrifice the good of the culture for personal gain—admired in the West as a driven personality that can think outside of the cultural box—or the man who claims to be rooted in culture but entices others to leave their cultural basis destroys the culture. What the West, in its elevation of the individual over the society, finds admirable and necessary for leadership is fatal to a communal culture.

Hyenas and ogres were the easiest and first to be won to the Christianity of the missionaries. And hyenas and ogres were the men the early missionaries appointed to be among the first chiefs.

One focus of the missionary world, that is touted even to this day, is the need to raise up strong Christian leadership to help a struggling society (in this case the Agikuyu) to follow a new direction. The more missionaries think this, the more they ensure the destruction of the peoples they claim to love and serve.

The teachings about leadership in the words of the Christ are not reflected in the missionary model of leadership. On the other hand, the teachings of the Christ on leadership, and the kind of leaders to avoid, is almost identical to the Agikuyu concept of avoiding ogres and hyenas—if not also rabbits and squirrels.

I am certain that there will be howls of protest about my handling of this subject, from all sides. It will take several more chapters to demonstrate my point on this matter.

When it comes to leadership, the Agikuyu had it right. The missionary world destroyed a far better understanding of leadership, in large part because they were willing accomplices of the colonial scheme.

And they are so vested in the Western concept of leadership, that they continue the carnage to this day.

CHAPTER 14

BRACKENHURST

My deepest apologies to those Kenyans who read this and are tired of my dwelling on only the Gikuyu. All Kenyan cultures have stories that compare well with this. Because I did my field studies interviewing Gikuyu elders, I am choosing to write about what I know best. In studying the Gikuyu, I also did some research with the Maasai, Dorobo, and a few others and asked lots of questions in my interviews about the Gumba. I am not trying to ignore other cultures but rather using what I know best to demonstrate what I believe is true throughout most of Kenya.

That said, this was one of the most difficult chapters for me to write.

SOME BACKGROUND

A *mukuyu* is a species of wild fig tree. A *gikuyu* is a giant wild fig tree. The original man of the Agikuyu creation story was a man named Gikuyu. Generally, the people of the original Gikuyu are called Agikuyu, an individual is called a Gikuyu, and the language is Gikuyu. Today, all these terms have generally melded into a single word, Kikuyu. But out of respect for the elders I interviewed, I am using these terms, the best I can, the way they used them.

For a long time, stretching back long before colonialism, there has always been a fundamental division among the Agikuyu. I will try to explain at least one aspect of this division. This is a difficult topic and one that has caused much grief in the culture. I will try to explain this division without adding fuel or fanning flames.

For the Americans among us, the United States in the eighteen hundreds had a similar division. There were two basic Americans. The first were the ones tied generally to the original colonies. Many of these were the American version of blue bloods, sort of the old-school elites who remained in their historical settings, content and unmotivated to adventure beyond their own original American territories, the colonial East Coast.

The second type of Americans were the ones who headed west under the heading of Manifest Destiny, the idea of a divine mandate to create a continuous civilization of European (white) America from sea to sea.

Often these two Americans were conflicted over what it meant to be an American, what freedom meant, what laws, if any, should govern a *free* man. The same division still exists in the United States, but the geography of the division has changed.

Now before I make the comparison, let me quickly say, no Gikuyu wants to be compared to Americans. Especially the expansionist mindset that destroyed Native American cultures in a merciless zeal that was and is appalling to say the least. Let me make the comparison and then judge me as you see fit.

BACK TO THE COMPARISON

There was also a divine mandate built into the creation stories of the Agikuyu. The Creator who spoke to the original man named Gikuyu showed him the land that lay between four mountains and told him that this was the land given to him to garden and protect. As the Agikuyu clans grew in numbers, they slowly expanded throughout the area that was shown to Gikuyu—their own Manifest Destiny.

Here is where the comparison falls apart.

There were several strict principles about land purchasing that were built into the Agikuyu belief system. I will mention two. First, any land that was not purchased between a willing seller and a willing buyer was considered stolen. Second, a land transaction could only occur between a Gikuyu man as seller and a Gikuyu man as buyer. A Gikuyu could never buy or sell any land from or to anyone other than a Gikuyu.

Much of the land that was purchased as the Gikuyu expanded came from the Maasai, a seminomadic culture; a hunter-gatherer community loosely called the N'dorobo; and the Gumba, a small Batwa, or Pygmy, culture. The Gikuyu used to call the Gumba "fierce children."

SIDEBAR

I am told there are several places in the Gikuyu highlands where one can still see the tunnels that were the entrances to the "fierce children's" underground homes. I was never fortunate enough to see one of those sites, but they should be national landmarks. If the owners of the land are looking for income, and advertised, it would become a tourist destination for other Kenyans, and international tourists very quickly. Politics being the dirty bastard that it is, such an enterprise, however, would likely become the target of greed.

While the existence of the Gumba is well known among the Agikuyu (and other Kenyan people), for a long time Western "experts" generally called stories of the Gumba myths. In the Western mind, nothing is true unless a white person has seen it. Don't dare to challenge me on this, or I will turn my Errant friends on you, as they have reams of examples that demonstrate exactly what I just said. I can give several personal examples of my own on this subject as well, if necessary.

The Gumba seem to have disappeared just before the advent of colonialism. The Gikuyu describe this as "swallowing them." As they expanded, they swallowed large portions of other cultures, or in the case of the Gumba, it seems they swallowed the entire culture. Many Gikuyu who are related to the Maasai are very tall, but there are several areas where the Gikuyu tend to be noticeably short (at least when I was there in the sixties and seventies). I have always thought this was because the people in those areas are not too distantly related to the Gumba.

BACK TO THE HISTORY LESSON

So, for a purchase to occur between a Gikuyu buyer and a Maasai, N'dorobo, or Gumba, the non-Gikuyu must first be a willing seller. Second, the non-Gikuyu seller had to go through a ritual where the seller was adopted into an Agikuyu clan—in theory the seller remained both a member of their original culture and a Gikuyu. A sort of dual citizenship if you will. In almost every case, a purchase included a marriage between a buyer (or one of his sons) and a daughter of the seller.

In many cases, it was more advantageous to be an Agikuyu than a member of one of the three other groups, and most (or all) dual citizens remained loyal to the Agikuyu. Many sales occurred precisely because a family from a neighboring culture wanted to join the Gikuyu. Today there are many Gikuyu men and women who have a parent, grandparent, or great-grandparent that are N'dorobo, Maasai, or Gumba. This is such a fascinating part of their history and is very much characterized by one of their sacred trees—the Mugumo tree. The Mugumo tree often grows when a bird leaves its seed in the crook of a branch of a host tree. Through a fascinating process, the Mugumo tree slowly takes over the host tree until the host tree disappears and all that is left is the Mugumo tree. The Mugumo swallows the host tree.

There are two types of Gikuyu, those who remain and live in the original homelands of the first generations of clans and those who grab the mantle of their Manifest Destiny and slowly purchase land, spreading toward the four mountains.

The first are the purists. They have the most consistent set of stories, folklore, and historical memory. In my interviews during my field study, they were by far the most consistent in recounting their traditions and historical memory. The second type of Gikuyu spread out in their quest to occupy the entirety of the area between the four mountains, purchasing land and intermarrying with their new neighbors. The further one goes into the expansion lands, the further removed the people are from their original stories and the more likely they become confused with the culture that they expanded into.

A child, for instance, of a Maasai woman turned Gikuyu could easily be taught practices and stories from both cultures. In my interviews with Gikuyu elders in these areas, I was amazed at how little these elders really knew about their own traditional stories and how much they believed was part of Gikuyu tradition was, in reality, Maasai or other traditions I did not know. I am told that the purest Gikuyu call the Gikuyu in some of these areas a term which basically means Gikuyu-Maasai because of the disconnect they see in them.

GETTING CLOSER TO MY POINT

At the onset of colonialism, the Gikuyu were just expanding into an area of the Kenyan highlands called Tigoni. This area includes a town now called Limuru.

The occupants of the Limuru-Tigoni area were the N'dorobo, the hunter-gathering community. They occupied the heavily forested areas that extended to the upper edge of the Great Rift Valley and down the slopes to a shelf about halfway down called the Okijabe. Their territory extended even farther, down to the valley floor to the beginning of the Maasai land. I believe there was a site in the Limuru area where the Gikuyu and Maasai traditionally held a market and traded or bartered for peace on the neutral N'dorobo lands. But at this time, the N'dorobo were beginning to sell properties to the Agikuyu, as described above, and they were quickly being swallowed by the Gikuyu.

SIDEBAR

The N'dorobo have a very mysterious past. Culturally, they reach back well before most of the present majority cultures began to occupy what is now Kenya. However, throughout the years, many people from cultures like the Maasai and Agikuyu, upon losing their status among their own people, joined the N'dorobo, and a significant sharing of cultures occurred. Many N'dorobo in the areas I am describing were former Maasai, as the Maasai culture was the easiest in which one could lose status (and a Maasai-N'dorobo could regain status and rejoin the Maasai as well). Because of this, the N'dorobo between the Maasai and Gikuyu tended to speak their own version of Maasai (Maa) with only trace remnants of their original language still intact.

Among the many tragedies of colonial history in Kenya was that the N'dorobo (now called Dorobo), of the areas that I have described, were forced by the colonial invaders to leave their lands and march across the valley floor to another mountain range on the other side of the valley where other Dorobo lived. This story has yet to be fully told. Much of the remaining land became the property of the Queen herself—it was now "empty and abandoned" land, of course!

BACK TO GETTING TO THE POINT

Among the properties being purchased from the N'dorobo by the Agikuyu in the Tigoni area as colonialism was encroaching elsewhere was a prize piece of land ideal for farming. It was purchased by at least four Agikuyu families (perhaps more).

It was not long before missionaries appointed a chief in the area.

A white settler wanted the land now being turned into farmland by the four Gikuyu families. The process was easy. The white farmer purchased the land from the chief (the representative of the Gikuyu people to the colonial powers). The chief's task was to use any means necessary to get the Gikuyu families off the land. He could use some of the purchase price if he wanted, but of course, the more money he spent, the less he kept for himself. So, the equivalent of pennies on the dollar were offered. Accepting the offer would immediately impoverish these otherwise wealthy Gikuyu landowners.

I am sorely tempted to tell the story of two of these landowners here—I interviewed a son and a granddaughter—But that story will have to come later or in another book.

For now, please remember that the chiefs appointed by the missionaries were, from the Agikuyu perspective, hyenas and ogres. Their god was their belly, and they were not in their positions for the good of the Agikuyu but by virtue of their own appetites.

Let me hasten to add that there were some chiefs who were great and notable men who fought for the Agikuyu and are heroes to this day among the people. They were the exceptions.

BRACKENHURST

Here is what is written on the website of the "farm" that the white settlers then began to occupy in 1914:

In 1914, a farm began in the green hills of Tigoni. A place infamously known as "nothing but mist," Tigoni was a sanctuary for vibrant wildlife and dazzling forests.

Progressing from a farm, wartime getaway and golf-course into an environmentally aware hotel and conference centre, Brackenhurst has spent over a hundred years reconnecting with the tremendous beauty of its natural surroundings.

Known as "Three Trees Farm" due to the three large muna trees left standing on the property, Brackenhurst was begun with the intention of creating a coffee farm. However, with the start of World War One, the owners of the farm soon found themselves providing holidays for battle-weary British soldiers. This marked the beginning of Brackenhurst's heritage as a center for hospitality.

Surviving several decades, an earthquake, and a well-concealed leopard, Brackenhurst Hotel was bought by the Baptist Mission of Kenya in 1964. It began to use its beautiful grounds for team-building, conferencing, and adventuring. In 2001, Brackenhurst developed a strong relationship with Plants For Life, an NGO focusing on environmental conservation. As a result, a vast indigenous forest grew on Brackenhurst soil for the first time since 1914. The forest provides a habitat for the restoration of some of the natural wildlife that once abounded in Tigoni.

Now under the management of Muna Tree Holdings, Brackenhurst is proud of its rich history and direct connection to the land around it. We invite you to develop your own story while staying here, a place where muna trees rise out of mist. (retrieved May 2020)

WHITEWASHED HISTORY

Histories like this literally boils the blood of the fast-growing intellectual community in Kenya. Truly, nothing happens in Africa until a white person shows up. And the farm began in 1914. The hard work of at least four families that turned a rainforest into a farm—an incredible feat in those days—well before 1914 gets no honorable mention. Nor is mentioned the fact that the original Gikuyu farmers who purchased the land from the N'dorobo—their deed or proof of ownership, under Agikuyu statute, still existing today—were forced off the land by good Christian chiefs appointed by missionaries.

I am still waiting for the Baptist Mission, who were so fortunate as to *legally* purchase the illegally purchased land—illegal by any modern law on earth—to show consideration for the families of the original owners who were intentionally disenfranchised by the colonial powers. Or, heaven forbid, give the land back.

I am almost willing to bet that there is not a single missionary who has enjoyed Brackenhurst over the years, worshiped God, went to life-changing seminars, rested there, who has any idea of the real history of Brackenhurst. For reasons beyond imagination, African history also begins, in the minds of most missionaries, with white people.

If the sole duty of the missionary was to spread the gospel where it was accepted and move on where it was rejected—the instructions of the Christ—knowing the history of Brackenhurst might not matter. This is because even where the message was accepted, the messenger would eventually move on—as the Christ instructed. The footprint of the messenger of the gospel would disappear with the next rain. But if one is going to ignore the instructions of the Christ and turn the endeavor into an occupation, then knowing the history matters.

I discovered one of the stories of the disenfranchised families in my first set of interviews and a second story in my fourth set of interviews. And I don't live in Kenya. My point is, it was not difficult to find these stories, and there are ones just like them all over Kenya. Among many of those places (perhaps most or all) that were grabbed are now missionary compounds—bringing a gospel that does not appear to care about the missionary's role in the history that brought Kenya to the point in which it exists today.

Most missionaries' understanding of history is limited to a brief orientation class regarding the country of their mission. Missionaries, as a rule, only feel accountable for what they themselves do or have done while they are in country. Few look any further back than that, and fewer still feel any obligation to do so. I find this is a disastrous mistake, because while missionaries continue to have historical amnesia, Africans are developing an increasing understanding of their history and what has been done to them.

Where is the apology for the missionary's role in history? Because they look no further back than their own calling, such an apology—and any restitution—is unlikely.

Happily, I suppose, the Roman Catholic Church has offered some apologies, as well as a pittance of land return. But this appears to be no more than a token olive branch. It does not look like repentance.

Remember the story of Zacchaeus in the Gospels? That is what repentance looks like. Ironically, the sycamore tree that he climbed up in is the same as the mukuyu tree, the tree that the Gikuyu are named after, a tree for worshipping God.

Perhaps it is time for missionaries to climb a mukuyu tree for themselves and look for Jesus.

CHAPTER 15

NEOCOLONIALISM

I asked several of my close friends in Kenya to read a draft of this book and invited feedback on what I have written. I feel I must address their concerns, so this essay was written and inserted here after I finished with the first draft.

Several of my Kenyan friends have mentioned to me that I am stopping short with the missionary and colonialism by not showing the connections between the missionary and current neocolonialism. My chapter on Brackenhurst was mentioned as one such missed opportunity.

MY HESITATION

Frankly, my greatest fear with this book is not what the missionary world will think of me but what damage I might inadvertently do to places like Kenya that are heavily burdened under neocolonialism.

One of the hardest lessons I learned over my years interviewing the elderly in the Kenyan highlands is how much damage has been done throughout Africa by *mzungus* (white people) like myself, even those with the most sympathetic of intentions.

Whatever one thinks of the white savior complex, all one need do is mention a specific about Africa and people want to send money or take off to some remote location and solve it. Even if it isn't a problem.

If there is any message that I want to convey it is that the opposite reaction is more honorable, that the highest amount of honor and respect one can give Africans is to simply leave them alone. They are fully capable of solving their own problems. We (white people and the Western complex) don't help by helping.

For this reason, my focus in this book has simply been on the need of missionaries to end their profession. I can speak with some level of sophistication about the missionary movement and feel that, in doing so, I cause little harm to an already harmed people.

It is hard, in my mind, as a white Westerner, to attempt to deal directly with neocolonialism, which is a very present and active crisis, without inadvertently encouraging two quite different ill effects.

First, those with the savior complex might be inclined to take it up as the basis for a new task to save Africa from itself.

Second, knowing full well that the so-called first world powers will not willingly release the cash cow of neocolonialism, the most likely historical outcome of an attack on its structures is the escalation of violence all over Africa as people attempt to end their oppression. I fear stirring the already boiling pot of discontent.

I hold to the gospel of peace, and stirring up violence, even what some might call *justified* violence, is not a part of my faith. I prefer people become part of a movement that lives as if those political powers don't exist and, at the same time, confronts false religion at every chance. This is the stuff that makes the Kingdom of God present on this earth.

I wish to follow the example of the Christ, who calls me to love my enemies even to my own death. God loves without distinction, and I do everything within my frail humanity to do the same.

But many, whom I dearly love, do not hold to my faith or accept my understanding of the gospel. Many more are simply in opposition to the very idea of the Christ, so wounded by the blunt force of Christianity. I honor and respect those people, and I wish no further harm to them.

So, I move forward cautiously.

NEOCOLONIALISM

Some who are less acquainted with the political, social, and economic pressures put on previous colonies and protectorates by the West may fail to appreciate how very real and onerous the economic and social upheaval continues to be. The staggering amount of money that flows out of Africa into the coffers of Europe alone guarantees that without structural revolution the future for Africa looks bleak. In the end, the definition of neocolonialism usually describes the use of economic, political, cultural, or other pressures to control or influence other countries, especially former dependencies.

Clearly, as my African friends suggest, missionaries support the leading dual edge of the neocolonial spear—foreign aid and conservation. And because of this, the gospel is just as hindered now as with colonialism.

I am aware of several missionary programs stationed around East Africa designed to teach Africans environmentally sustainable farming, tree reforestation, and the like.

Imagine the arrogance of this in the mind of an African who has any historical memory. Africans have been farming or raising livestock successfully and sustainably for thousands of years. They have long since learned the sustainable use of resources in any given region, including the maintenance of an abundant and robust wildlife unmatched anywhere on earth.

Without missing a beat, those that destroyed African lives, took their lands, and marginalized them into cycles of poverty are suddenly experts in saving what only a short while ago they themselves systematically destroyed.

The hubris of this is beyond comprehension.

BRACKENHURST

In February of 2020, Brackenhurst hosted an international conservation conference called Pathways Africa.

In the minds of those fighting the racist undertones of conservation in Africa, this conference is seen—in the words of one of my Kenyan friends—as "a confluence of Christianity and conservation colonialism. It is awful the way they are trying to cleanse their sins against humanity with an obsession about biodiversity."

Here is a blurb from the conference website:

> While the area is historically colonialist, there has been a big push by local organizations in the last two decades to restore Limuru's biodiversity and ecosystems to their pre-colonial state—most notably by Plants for Life International and the Brackenhurst Learning Center. In collaboration, the two Limuru-based organizations have worked to convert 60 acres of silent eucalyptus plantation back to indigenous forest. Over the last 19 years, their efforts have successfully restored 40 hectares of indigenous forest with 1,000 native species of trees and plants, resulting in major positive impacts on the area's biodiversity. (retrieved May 2020)

Once again, no mention of the Agikuyu before colonialism—apparently the land simply didn't exist before that travesty. There is no hint or mention of restoring the land to its human owners, who know fully well how to preserve and sustain the area.

This is Western neocolonialism.

CONSERVATION

There are two views of conservation imposed on Africa from the West. One view sees the solution (to the problem manufactured by the West) to be fortress conservation. This is where Africans are forced off their traditional homelands and into a marginalized existence and poverty in the name of animal preservation.

On this subject, I strongly encourage reading *The Big Conservation Lie* by John Mbaria and Mordecai Ogada. This book will pain and anger most people, and well it should.

On the other Western view of conservation, game management, I am going to make a more personal appeal.

Like many missionaries and children of missionaries, I grew up hunting. I acquired a hunting license from the game department, a Western controlled department even in postcolonial Kenya. The professional hunters in those days were almost exclusively white people with African helpers. We did think that we were part of a necessary management, which involved culling specific species from certain areas to maintain wildlife health.

In a sense, this worked. White people were slowed in their progressive overkilling of African wildlife by hunting limitations—while African hunters were simply redefined as poachers.

The absurdity of it all is that, at the time, it did not occur to me to put together what I already knew, that most Africans opposed hunting wildlife and, when they hunted, it was almost always by necessity.

It is Africans and their traditions of cohabitation that have given the world the most abundant and diverse range of species on earth. The Western world has no history that can match Africa on this point.

Yet, we are there managing their world and devastating it at the same time.

I am embarrassed that I did not see this absurdity as a child, in my context surrounded by a Western culture that was, in its own mind, saving Africa—both literally and spiritually.

I still am a hunter, and I make no apologies for it. However, I know that Africa has its own ethics about hunting and wildlife, which is far superior to anything the West has ever conceived. They do not separate humans from wildlife, and when left side by side, both thrive with little conflict.

Again, please consider reading *The Big Conservation Lie*. This subject is not in my purview.

I want to finish this essay with a parable, of sorts. I wrote for another son of missionaries who was thinking of going hunting in Africa for old time's sake. He still maintained the notion that his hunting was good and helped Africa, a notion we missionary kids in those days all learned from the colonial and neocolonial world we grew up in.

AN ALLEGORY

Let's pretend.

Let's suppose you are a hunter in America, one of eight hundred thousand or so. Let's say all your guns are taken away (or bows or other weapons).

Let's say if you are found with a weapon, or appeared to be hunting, or took your dog, cat, or pet goat on a walk in an area where wild animals exist, you would be arrested, lose property, and be fined enough to bankrupt you. That's if you're lucky. The rangers have the power to shoot you on sight.

Let's say that hunting is still legal in most of America. But it is only legal for certain foreigners. Elite Africans are invited to come and hunt in your former backyard and lands.

That stream that runs one hundred yards from your house is protected, so you can't go near it, but those African sport hunters can go to the river, sit on the banks, and shoot anything that comes down to drink.

But don't worry, those elite Africans can only take the trophy and skin with them. They donate the meat to the nearest town, so you get to eat wild game after all! They know you will be grateful that they have kept you fed one more day. Of course, if you live in a town of any size, your cut of that donated meat won't be enough to make a snack.

You can go on hunts. Lucky you! You can drive vehicles for those elites, you can set up camps for them, you can carry their guns and tree stands (you won't get shot if you carry their guns and don't run away). You even—get this—you even can skin, gut, salt, and carry everything back to camp for them! They will teach you to cook their food, so you are more useful. After all, the elites believe that it is always a good thing to take care of a local. It is fortunate that you get to be their "local."

It is easy to understand the rules. If you are white and you are found around a dead animal in the wild, you are a poacher and are subject to being shot on sight. You are a poacher unless the animal was shot by one of those kind and generous elite Africans, who are, you may remember, going to give your town the meat.

When elite Africans shoot an animal in America, especially an exotic one, it makes them a hunter, not a poacher.

The elites pay an extremely high price for the hunt, but they can smile, resting assured by the literature that explains how portions of the proceeds go to the local Americans in the area where they hunt. As it turns out, the proceeds that go to the local Americans are nothing more than the tiny portions of game meat that are given out.

They might also dig a well for you. The fresh water you used to get from the waterfall or dam is now a private lodge, and you cannot access it or get water from it. Most likely, the hosts of the elite Africans—elite Africans themselves—have shown the proposed well sight to hunters for the last decade, announcing their intention to build a well there for the local Americans. Of course, even without equipment, that well could have been dug in two days. But mineral rights belong to the elite Africans, so no American can safely dig the well for themselves.

Once the well is complete, the water is given a cursory test and the well is turned over to the Americans. It will quickly become contaminated, but no matter. It is better than having to go to another town to get bottled water because, if you remember, you can't go to the river.

The rest of the proceeds from hunts goes to the estates of elite Africans who run the professional outfits that host the elite African hunters who come to America for sport.

And the true advantage of being an elite African host of elite African sport hunters is you become a hero as a conservationist, one who saves animals from extinction by separating dangerous Americans from their wildlife. Money pours into your war chest from animal lovers all over the world who wish Americans could just learn, or perhaps just stop having babies.

If I must explain that this is exactly what happens in Africa in reverse, then you may be an idiot—as I confess I once was.

I have asked my Kenyan friends to provide a list of books they feel best describe the African experience of neocolonialism. Please find this list in appendix 1.

CHAPTER 16

COMMERCE

Many missionaries, especially ones who work in Africa, look at David Livingstone as a champion and forerunner of the modern missionary endeavor. Livingstone was championed for his vision of "commerce, Christianity, and civilization." These solutions were primarily promoted, by him, to end slavery in Africa. It is extremely hard to separate the man from the myths and legends that surround him.

Less than a decade after Livingstone's death, the Scramble for Africa began, as well as the Golden Age of Missions.

The founder of the mission society that I grew up in while a child in Kenya, Peter Cameron Scott, first knelt at the grave of David Livingstone before boarding a ship and finally arriving at Mombasa to begin a mission endeavor. Scott's vision grew out of Livingstone's words. Scott's vision was to establish a chain of mission stations from Mombasa to Lake Chad in the Central African Republic. He wanted to establish mission stations along known and suspected slave routes and to disrupt them through the three Cs of Livingstone's vision: commerce, Christianity, and civilization.

There were mission societies already in parts of Africa before Livingstone, but a decided shift took place after Livingstone's vision captured the Christians of the West.

Livingstone's vision carried along with it a blindness to any indication that Africa, in general, already had a functioning commerce, a sophisticated civilization (civilizations), and its own Christian tradition, which was in place well before the message had reached Europe.

Commerce, at least the Western version of it, came roaring into Africa on the heels of colonialization. The immediate result was the abundance of wealth sent back to the fledgling nations in Europe. This created the desired effect, and Europe's economies were launched into hyperdrive.

Of course, Africa's own economies were destroyed in the process, and the former victims of the slave trade soon came to understand that their entire cultures had become vassals of Europe. Instead of the slavery of individuals, it became the slavery of a continent.

Do not think for a moment that this is an overstatement. The direct and indirect genocide and subjugation of Africa by Europeans during and after the Scramble is unconscionable and undeniable.

The audacity of including civilization as part of a missionary endeavor is not only in complete contradiction to the gospel of the Christ, the missionary world has forever blighted Christianity by its association with Western civilization.

But let's return to commerce. It is difficult for me to put myself back into the mid- and late eighteen hundreds and understand what commerce really meant to Livingstone and the early missionaries back then. It was a time when commerce was beginning to deconstruct in the West, and two new ideas emerged (both of Western origin) and ultimately divided from each other—Marxist socialism and a new definition of capitalism. Both ideas were the byproduct of the West's two industrial revolutions in the early and then late eighteen hundreds.

Before industrialization, these ideas of commerce and the worker would not have been incompatible. The majority populations of the Western nations were farmers, or shopkeepers, trade merchants, and other small owner-operators, who lived in small interdependent communities.

In many ways, the preindustrial communities and farmlands in the West were both capitalist and socialist at the same time. By the end of the eighteen hundreds, the two ideas had become incompatible. But they were incompatible because independent, self-governing states had reached their zenith following the gradual decline of empires and sovereign kingdoms. Europe, especially, was ravaged and broken in the aftermath of the Napoleonic wars. Fledgling states were just reemerging as sovereign and independent nations.

In my view, the real issue with economics in the West is not about the development of a new model but the inability to let go of post-feudalistic expansionism. What saved Europe from the economic disaster of the feudalist system was the first ships returning from exotic destinations loaded with a new basis of wealth.

It was quickly discovered that by simply taking the resources of others, and later exploiting the labor of others through slavery and colonialism, that a nation could stabilize itself economically. Even with the so-called end of colonialism, the Western world is still incapable of self-sufficiency without exploiting others beyond its borders. Now, of course, more gentle words are used like "national interests."

So try to think about this: a civilization that has never succeeded economically (be it capitalist or communist) without expansionism and exploitation thinks itself uniquely positioned to introduce commerce to ancient civilizations that long before learned to exist economically side by side without exploitation and with free and open trade by individuals.

Livingstone's three Cs became an utter disaster on all three counts. The conversion Protestant missionaries failed the most miserably at commerce. I have never met a missionary who has had any real background in business. If such a person exists or existed, the policy of most conversion Protestant mission societies discourages the actual practice of commerce.

Ironically, it seems the Apostle Paul would have been discouraged from tentmaking in the faith-support philosophies of many Protestant societies.

Sadly, much of Africa is now divided by economic theories that began in the West. There are capitalist leaning countries, socialist leaning countries, and communist leaning countries. This separation of theories was never necessary in African civilizations.

Historically, African societies have always been both able to engage in free trade with each other while being fully communalist societies. It is only in the dichotomist West that these two ideas stand at odds with each other.

Contrary to Livingstone's idea, the three Cs, commerce, Christianity, and civilization, taken together were the last thing that Africa needed, and the West, indeed, was the last civilization qualified to provide them. Yet, this was the clarion call of the modern Golden Age of Missions.

It was wrong then, and it is wrong now.

CHAPTER 17

NEVER LET THEM GO

There was a saying among the traditional Gikuyu, an instruction, given at the coming of age rituals, given again at marriage, and given again before and during each child born into the family. It was included in songs and dances and folktales. The essence of the saying is, "Hold on to your children and never let them go, never let them go."

No matter how young or old a child was, among a parent's chief responsibilities was to keep their children close to them. For life.

This was the norm among the Gikuyu until missionaries, under the watchful eyes of colonialism, decided that they knew better.

A little bit of the Agikuyu perspective must have rubbed off on me in my childhood. As a parent, I did not want my children ever being under the tutelage of another—we homeschooled. It was several years before we allowed anyone other than family to keep our children. When I worked (I owned a trucking company), I often had one of my two boys riding with me. When it came to sports, we were always directly involved and participated—we tried to always hold on to our children.

Ultimately, I failed at this task. Fourteen years of depression made my ideal impossible. All in all, however, I am in complete sympathy with the Agikuyu perspective on raising their children.

As a believer, however, I don't think my perspective was biblical, nor was it unbiblical. I certainly don't think homeschooling is biblical or unbiblical. Neither do I think the Agikuyu understanding of raising children is biblical or unbiblical. Though, the Agikuyu's perspective is certainly reflected throughout the Hebrew scriptures, so if one were to make an argument for biblical, they certainly would have a leg up on almost anything that is considered normative child-rearing in Western culture.

One is hard put to come up with a biblical perspective on child raising. Though Christianity has spent (or wasted) thousands of hours writing books, giving seminars, and hosting retreats on what is biblical child raising. Biblical is a word that should not exist, as it assumes something about the sacred texts of believers that the Bible never claims for itself—that it is some sort of how-to or training manual.

As cultural shifts took place in the history of the Hebrews, so did the hints on how they raised their children. If anything, biblical is to raise your child within the context of your own culture, and if you are a follower of Christ, then parent as one who lives under the principles of the best expression of God possible, the Christ—"If you have seen Me, you have seen the Father."

Yes, I know in the book of Proverbs there is the proverb (often poorly translated) that says something like, "He who spares the rod hates his son." To the Western mind, the rod is an instrument of punishment. To the shepherd, the rod and staff were the tools of the shepherd trade. They were never used as instruments of punishment. As David said in the Psalms, "Your rod and your staff, they comfort me."

Go study the use of a rod and staff in ancient shepherding techniques. You will find that they never punished, they guided wayward sheep in a better direction, or rescued or calmed a sheep in trouble. They were instruments of gentle love. The point is every culture expects parents to guide their children and help them when they are in trouble. Those are instruments of gentle love. The idea that a rod on the back of one's child is what is in view here is an absurdity.

I am going to try to be very general here. Americans have a vastly different idea of what child raising should look like than did the Agikuyu. Americans tend to believe in early education; they believe in getting their children into the best school possible; they believe that *not* sending their children to be under the tutelage of others is irresponsible and, in some cases, tantamount to child abuse. Again, I am generalizing. I know there are plenty of subculture Americans who do not send their children to be educated by strangers, but most do.

So, what is child abuse for a traditional Gikuyu (and was for myself) is responsible child raising for the average American. And vice versa. Sadly, in modern Kenya, including among the Gikuyu, a responsible parent sends their children off to boarding school. I'll return to boarding schools again in another missive, but for now, this change in the modern Gikuyu is an extreme leap from their traditional past.

If you need evidence that it was the education model imposed upon the Gikuyu that motivated this radical jump in parenting—look no further than the fact that *responsible* missionary parents routinely send their children to boarding school. Most American (and likely European) parents would consider this wrong, or at least abnormal, yet it has continued in the missionary world for over one hundred years.

Missionaries have told me that the change that occurred in the Gikuyu mindset was not only to be blamed on them. After all, colonialists, the white farming community, and whites after Kenyan independence routinely sent their children to boarding school. So, let's see, missionaries are willing to model the example of the colonialist? I thought the idea was to model the Christ that one claims to believe. Once again, the marriage between the missionary and the colonial powers is evident, even in education.

Now for most Gikuyu parents, there is no longer the call for holding on to their children and never letting them go. Not only are they sending their children to be under the tutelage of strangers but additionally sending them out of their household in the process. Today's Kenyan considers it the best type of parenting if they send their children to live in a different part of the country, to be raised and educated by complete strangers. This is an extreme that even many Americans, if they think about it, would consider unacceptable, perhaps appalling.

THE SHOE ON THE OTHER FOOT

Now, let's pretend for a moment that Gikuyu missionaries, with the backing of an oppressive and intrusive government, came to America and forced every American to adopt their perspective on child raising and education. Of course, they would be doing it for the good of the American! Of course, they would be ending systemic child abuse that is pervasive throughout the American culture. The Gikuyu, from their perspective of morality, would be doing the heathen Americans a service.

Those backward Americans would be forced to change. Of course, it would destroy their culture because educational systems are the backbone of all culture. But the culture should change, right? It is moral to force them to adopt another model of education because their culture is, after all, immoral.

Don't get me wrong, I do happen to think the American concept of education is wrong, and in some cases morally wrong—but remember, I happen to think the traditional Agikuyu understanding of education is based on the better principles. Remember too, however, when I howl and protest the American concept of education, I neither have nor want the power to enforce my ideas. That power, if enforced, would be an immoral imposition.

A SIDEBAR

The current perspective on education in the West is the birth child of the first and second industrial revolutions. Historically, the American and European ideas of education were much closer to the Agikuyu idea. I think this shift has done what may be irreparable harm to generations, including ours. It grieves me that Americans do not actively engage in understanding what their education is about and how it developed.

BACK TO THE SUBJECT AT HAND.

The point I hope I am making is that child raising is a mix of culture and, hopefully, good, loving parents. What is moral in one culture is immoral in another. Evil is when one culture imposes their ideas of education on another from a different culture. Yet, this precise imposition is exactly what missionaries have done, and continue to do. This is evil. And it is no longer just missionaries, it is part and parcel of most foreign aid.

CHAPTER 18

ONWARD CHRISTIAN CHILDREN

Try hard to imagine yourself an elder in a communal society. Imagine your position in that society. You have lived long enough to see life for what it is. You have accumulated knowledge, but more importantly, you have accumulated experience, and along with it, a modicum of that elusive thing called wisdom. Your culture puts a premium on wisdom, and you have earned a seat on the council.

Your culture values knowledge and values new ideas, but knowledge never trumps the experience that leads to wisdom. New knowledge seeks your wisdom and never the other way around.

Then children show up.

Sometimes they are a youth group from some woe-begotten church in the United States or Europe. Their youth leaders arranged the trip—to provide them with a *world view*. I am certain they had some sort of orientation on being sensitive in cross-culture communications, probably by some self-proclaimed expert on such communication. They might have been told to show respect to elders.

What do these children do? They might paint a church. They might sit around in circles getting selfies with little black children sitting on their laps, playing guitars and teaching songs about God. They might pray. And, most importantly, they might share their testimony. What, in fact, are these children doing there?

Soon enough, their world view has changed. These little skulls of mush go home forever changed by their experience. Most tragically, some are determined to go back to that world so full of need and to continue to help. They have learned the most important message possible, little black children in Africa need them to help, to teach, to educate, to impart, to spread knowledge.

CHILDREN TEACHING ELDERS

One question before I go on. How exactly does a child who lives in a culture that does not naturally respect elders for their wisdom show respect for an elder in a culture that does? The answer is simple. They do not, because they really have no idea what wisdom means, much less why to value one who has obtained some measure of it. And it is unlikely the expert that told them to show respect has any idea what wisdom is either.

If the self-proclaimed expert did have wisdom and did understand respect, they would never in their wildest dreams consider sending a child armed with some modicum of knowledge into a culture that values wisdom over knowledge. If they understood respect in the slightest, they would never send anyone into such a culture who was not themselves old and bent over a cane. This, at least, would show a modicum of respect.

Now, here is what those children are unknowingly doing. They are teaching that their Western culture, or Western Christian culture, is so superior, their knowledge of the Creator of All so elevated, that the Western culture can send their children to insult the fabric of another culture. A Western child by their presence and show of ministry makes it clear that they, as children, contain more wisdom than any elder in the community they descend upon. That is what these children are doing. It is the prime message, no matter what the intention.

Some of those children (too many, in fact) go to college and learn new knowledge and return to a place in the world where people's melanin is a bit darker than theirs. But even educated children are still children. They are still years from learning the hard lessons of life, much less the lessons of death. No matter how well trained they are, they can only impart knowledge without wisdom to communities who have lived for thousands of years elevating wisdom over knowledge. One can never learn wisdom from education.

No matter how much they have learned in their academics, they are still children. And their message to the elders of the community they come to help is the same: my knowledge trumps your wisdom.

There is no amount of respect one can show an elder that will overcome that message.

If this were a book on foreign aid, I would go in another direction. But this is about missionaries and their perceived purpose. Please show me the section in the scriptures that you quote about going to other cultures and *helping* them, much less sending your children to do so. Show me where the message that the Master taught comes with aid, technology, knowledge, and personal testimonies.

If the message you have cannot stand on its own without the trinkets of your culture and your *knowledge*, then your message is too weak to stand on its own.

If you think so little of other cultures that you think it is a good idea to send your children to them, in the name of your faith, then you are blinded by your profound sense of cultural superiority. Don't send your children and, in so doing, reinforce your bigotry in your children as well.

I remember a time, probably a decade ago, when I was in Kenya. I happened to be eating in a dining room with an American youth group that was just back from a trip to a nearby country. The boy sitting across from me was excited. He informed me that the people in that country were hungry to be taught the Bible. He was determined to go back and help them learn what the Bible said.

I asked him if he met any believers in that country that were my age (fifties at the time). Of course, he had.

I told him what it was like to be a Christian back in the seventies in the country that he had just visited—the torture, the mass killings of Christians, men forced to watch their families tortured to death to get them to renounce their faith. I told him that during that time of persecution, the country he visited was home to one of the fastest growing churches on earth. Torture and pain always begets believers.

I told him about a cycle of famines in the country, that believers had shriveled up and died in equal numbers to everyone else. They experienced that disappointment in a God that does not seem to care—a God whose promises seemed empty—that poverty of hope when the promises of protection seem to gut every promise that Christians are told to believe in. Still, believers my age thrived and still believed.

I asked this young American, who had never suffered torture, never experienced hunger, never lived through a day of true disappointment in God, I asked him what he could possibly teach from a book of knowledge to a person who had learned his faith alongside the wisdom of living a full and complicated life.

The young man did not appreciate my question. Or understand it. How could he? He lived in a culture where knowing more is key to everything. He only understood one thing as necessary—he needed to get more knowledge to teach more knowledge. Wisdom meant nothing. He did not understand that he was the one who needed to sit at the feet of those believers he sought to teach. That he had nothing to offer them. He was the one in need, not them.

It is a moral outrage to send children around the world to do—well—anything in the name of God. Why is the atrocity of this idea so lost on people? Why is it so noble for another generation of white saviors to be unleashed on this earth? Where is the gospel in that?

The answer I get most, from parents, youth leaders, short term missionary proponents, is how good these trips are for the children. Damn the consequences, it is good for the kids. Even if I agreed that going on overseas youth mission trips was a good thing for children, which I don't, shouldn't it matter more to find out if what they are doing is actually good for the people to whom they are sent? Are *we* that selfish?

The question of what is good for those of the intended mission, those the children are to teach, is something that neither the children, their parents, or the so-called initiators of these missions have even the basis of knowing. And the fact that some indigenous pastor or Christian leader invited them is not proof of anything. At least not proof of anything good.

Of course, there are many other questions to ask about this march of Christian children—like what are the economic impacts, or the dependency cycles created? But I'll leave further discussion on such questions in the hands of others more capable.

CHAPTER 19

NO DISTINCTIONS

I was in high school when the Rift Valley Academy, the missionary boarding school I attended, made a rule.

It seemed that there had been some skirmishes of sorts between the students of my school—a school primarily for missionary children—and the students of the nearby Kijabe High School—a school for local Africans. That fact alone that there were two separate high schools speaks volumes.

The new school rule made it clear that there was to be no more fraternization between our school and the African high school. For those of us who had spent most or all our lives among Africans, we felt much more in common with the students from Kijabe than students at Rift Valley. On personal grounds, the rule, if any students were inclined to pay attention to it, was onerous and immediately heightened tensions between the schools.

I lived in Kijabe. My home was right next to the entrance to the Kijabe High School—where many of my best friends went.

The new rule incensed me on several levels. The primary issue for me, however, was the fact that a school for the children of missionaries to Africa was being kept from association with its next-door neighbors. Apparently loving one's neighbors was out of the question in the absurd context of the missionary boarding school.

My friends at Kijabe High School took the rule very personally—and well they should have.

I, along with a couple of my Kijabe High School friends, devised a plan. I went to the managers of the mission station and asked permission to use the mission conference room once a week for a Bible study. Of course, they were delighted, imagining, I think, that a few Rift Valley Academy students wanted to study together. Permission was granted.

I circulated invitations at my school, and my African friends made invites at theirs.

The first night of Bible study was standing room only, filled with faces from both schools.

I don't remember much about the content of those Bible studies, but I do remember the opening topic on the first night. I read a passage from the book of Galatians that, loosely translated, says, "There are no Jews or Gentiles, no slaves or free, no males or females, for there are to be no distinctions in the Christ called Jesus."

From that reading, I asked on what basis was there any distinction between those of us from Kijabe High and those of us from Rift Valley. This began a rigorous discussion that lasted many meetings.

When the administration at Rift Valley Academy heard about our Bible study, and the blatant fraternization between students of RVA and Kijabe High School, their hands were tied. I hope they were embarrassed by the audacity of the rule.

After I left Kenya, I was told by another Rift Valley student that the Bible study lasted for several years after those of us who started it were gone.

CHAPTER 20

BOARDING SCHOOLS

I want to revisit the boarding school subject again from a different point of view.

But first a bit of disclosure.

While I attended a boarding school for eleven years, I was never an actual boarder at the school. My family lived in the same town as the school, so I lived at home while I attended. Certainly, my own personal experiences did a lot to shape my opinion of boarding schools, very personal experiences of abuse, sexual and otherwise, and being the friend of other boarding school students. However, the truth is, I never spent a night in a boarding school dorm.

Some have told me that I have no right to judge, since I never lived in a dorm. Perhaps this is fair. I also have never murdered anyone. I suppose, by this logic, I should also not judge the act of murder either?

A GIFT FROM THE EMPIRE

The biggest exporter of the idea of boarding schools, without question, is Britain. The history of these schools goes back over one thousand years on the British Isles. The British Empire, as it expanded across the world in its diabolical colonial crusade, brought boarding schools along with it, first to educate its own children and then to educate the brightest minds among those who fell prey to its power.

Ironically, the best literature that I have seen about the long-term damage of boarding schools also comes from England. Boarding School Syndrome (BSS) is among the terms psychologists use to describe the damage that lasts throughout adulthood. Thankfully, in some circles, this damage is increasingly recognized.

I am amazed at the similarities between what is described as BSS and the recognized characteristics of what are called TCKs (third-culture kids) and MKs (missionary kids). The glaringly obvious difference to me is that BSS is considered a damaging condition that lasts a lifetime and TCKs and MKs who exhibit those same characteristics consider themselves to be a part of a community of a similar-minded people with a unique outlook on the life around them. Some of those outlooks are indeed unique, and sometimes positively so, but many or most are, in my view, clearly part of the same psychological pathology as BSS.

Rather than bore you regarding the emerging literature about BSS, I would encourage those interested to look for themselves.

I will only point out that a significant percent of TCKs and MKs, if not the vast majority, were or are also boarding school kids, so the similarities in pathologies should be expected. Of course, those who only experienced boarding schools for a few years, especially at the end of their high school years, may have little or no experience with most of the pathologies.

For England, the percent of boarding school students rarely exceeded 1 percent. What makes this significant in England is that the 1 percent of students generally mirrors the children of the highest class in that society.

Of the colonial victims of England, there are many countries who now have boarding school systems that far exceed 1 percent of students, and many of these countries now consider it the height of parental responsibility to put their children into a boarding school. Many parents will work and struggle to put their children into these schools that are well beyond the parents' means. So while the monstrous empire that began it all is finally recognizing the damage these institutions have done to generations, the colonized victims of the monster continue to follow its example, in hopes of elevating their youth to a better life, traumatizing their children for life in the process.

FORSAKING ALL FOR GOD

There is a period of American history sometimes called the Third Great Awakening. It is roughly a period covering the late eighteen hundreds and early nineteen hundreds. This period, in terms of American Christianity, saw the hardening and separation of the Christian left and right, and many of the debates that began in those decades still linger today.

I bring this up because part of this period was what became known as the Sawdust Revivals or Sawdust Trail Meetings. It was so named because big tents were put up, or barns used, and the floors were covered in sawdust. People, it was said, came down the "sawdust trail" to the front of the congregation for repentance and conversion.

A somewhat popular (and thankfully short-lived) idea that came out of those revivals was that to commit to Jesus meant to forsake all, including family, to follow Christ; it became popular among several segments of Christianity for parents to put their children in orphanages or boarding schools so that the parents could serve God full-time. This concept was taken from an extreme understanding of a teaching of the Christ on the so-called Sermon on the Mount.

This movement coincided with the Golden Age of Missions, as soft imperialists opened the doors for missionaries all over the expanding colonial world. The birth of almost every major missionary boarding school occurred during this period. Armed with the call to be dedicated wholly to God, along with the ongoing colonial propagation of boarding schools, it was a match made in hell.

It was not long before American Christians that were influenced by those sawdust revivals began to realize the damage that was being done to their children, and it was, in fact, a short-lived movement. The missionary world continued and continues. Damn the statistics, the God show must go on.

A VISCERAL RESPONSE

This aspect is especially personal for me and my family. One of the primary reasons that our family lived in the same place as a boarding school was that my father was one of those damaged children. He was put in an orphanage so that his parents could serve God. I don't know many details, but I know enough to know that the things that happened to my father scarred him for life, and the effects and damage to him made our home a dysfunctional and abusive environment. Of course, many homes throughout the world are dysfunctional and abusive, but to justify it in the name of God is exceptionally repugnant.

It was not long before my father's parents realized what they had done, and they removed him from the orphanage. Every missionary parent that sends their child to boarding school so that they can serve God does so in a state of cognitive dissonance. Every fiber of a parent's being knows that sending their child away to be raised and taught by strangers for the formative time of their child's life is aberrant parenting.

I have vitriolic anger at the very idea of a missionary boarding school. I began my separation from historical Christianity because of this issue. In case that is misunderstood, I have never left following the Christ, but I see little in common with the teachings of Jesus and the teachings and history of Christianity. My point is, I cannot be objective on this subject because of how personal it is to me.

THE DICHOTOMY

Stepping away from missionary boarding schools and looking at boarding schools that are now all over Kenya, the damage that is being done to a generation of Kenyan children is becoming clear. Not just the damage of the syndrome that is prevalent in children who attend boarding school, but the casual way that boarding-school children in Kenya accept the abuse and sexual deviancy as an all too common part of their education. I have heard countless stories and seen the numbed faces of children who have created a dichotomy in their lives to separate themselves from those experiences. That dichotomy will be with them for life.

One of the most serious ideas in scripture is the idea of emulating the Christ. "Follow me as you see the Christ in me." The point, of course, is to follow the Christ, not the person. How exactly is sending your children away to a boarding school so you can serve the Christ an example for others to follow?

The boarding school concept does not come from the Christ. For many, it is a kind of hell that lives with them for a life. It is a disgrace that such an idea as boarding schools ever entered the minds of missionary societies. And it is ever more evil that missionary societies continue to operate boarding schools for any reason.

CHAPTER 21

CULTURE AND MEMORY

In my interviews in Kenya, I talked to several elderly men and women around the Kijabe missionary station where I was born and raised.

A close Gikuyu friend of mine who traveled with me on some of my interviews urged me to write a history of the small town from the point of view of the Africans who lived there—not the missionaries, not the African church leaders, but the local Africans who lived and often struggled just to survive there. Despite my reluctance to take on the task, my friend egged me on every time we met with another elder near the station.

As he introduced me, his habit became to request that the elder tell me about the missionary promise to Kijabe. It was quite telling how many elders knew exactly what my friend was talking about.

According to the small chorus of voices that I interviewed, the early missionaries invited Gikuyu Christians from various parts of the highlands to come join them at Kijabe for a new kind of village, a village where missionary and Gikuyu lived together as one community. There would be no distinctions. Kijabe would be a light to Africa of the harmony that can exist between believers of all backgrounds.

While all the elders told slightly different versions of how this promise of equality was broken through the years, all agreed that this promise had been made to them in the beginning. They are still waiting for signs for it to be fulfilled.

They pointed out how, in the early days, their children went to school together, but that soon ended, and African children were separated from the missionaries' children. They pointed out how they used to have herds of cattle and sheep on the station, but the missionaries soon put an end to that. Housing for the missionaries was materially Western and became more and more separated from allowable housing for the Africans. Africans went to work as employees for the missionaries' projects and as groundskeepers and cooks for the missionary school. Businesses and allowable merchandise were restricted, and station fees made it onerous for locals to operate independently without working for the missionaries and their endeavors.

When at last, over seventy years later, the reins of Kijabe were turned over to the national church, Africa Inland Church. The distinction continued, this time with new levels of privilege. African church leaders imitated the separateness of the missionaries and distinguished themselves from locals. Church imposed local taxes and power bills became even more usurious.

Though I never had the heart to see if it was true, the church leaders, I am told, began to build houses that were even grander than many missionaries and totally out of the reach of the limited economic capabilities of the community—the so-called community. Kijabe has become a money machine for the AIC, which loosely defines itself as a ministry.

My friend was a casualty of that church money machine. He was fired from his career because of church politics, not because of his work but because the political machine of the African Inland Church had someone else in mind for the position. Before my friend passed away, he took the missionaries' failed promise very personally.

In the 120 years that missionaries have been at Kijabe, I would wager that few beyond the original missionaries ever heard of this promise at the inception of the station. In fact, I have every reason to doubt that the current crop of missionaries would feel any responsibility for such a promise made so long ago.

This is the difference in memory between an individualistic culture like the West and a communal culture. Africans (at least the elderly) still remember. Missionary memory tends to be myopic. They only remember and feel responsible for their little slot of time in history. Resentment and hurt on one side are met by blindness and willful ignorance on the other. And it is not a myopia limited to missionaries; it is their Western culture.

What remains true of both missionaries as they were in the colonial era and missionaries today is the lopsided idea that for Kijabe to become a community, all the significant change must come from the locals. After all, the historical idea of the African as a heathen was entrenched in missionary culture early.

When I was looking through the archives at Wheaton College during my graduate work, I began to run across letters and photos from the first wave of missionaries who stationed at Kijabe. Clearly the promise of equality that the Agikuyu elderly felt had been made to their parents and grandparents was from this first wave of missionaries.

At the time, I was looking for things more related to my thesis, but I made note of events of interest about the place where I was born. These things revealed much about the context in which such a promise might have been made.

I mentioned a letter in a previous essay in which a missionary wrote to her supporters and praised God that some girls in the mission school called the Kijabe Girls School had successfully been hidden from their parents when their parents came looking for them. These girls, rescued from their heathen culture, were dressed in Western clothing, and all their cultural markings were removed or covered. According to the missionary, the girls were so well disguised that their own parents couldn't recognize them.

Amazingly, the missionaries' moral indignation against the heathens and their practices gave them justification to literally take babies, and especially young girls, away from their parents and community to raise a generation of native Christians. Yet all around them, colonialization was displacing innumerable people, taking their lands and giving them only the choice of being tenant labor for the white farmers on their own traditional land or leaving and suffering immediate poverty.

Soon Africans were no longer allowed to attended Rift Valley Academy in Kijabe but the children of white farmers were still welcome. It was not until thirty years later when the hedonistic atrocities among the white farms in an area of Kenya called Happy Valley that the school was forced to change their policy no longer accept the children of the white settlers.

What kind of community is it that separates itself from the African believers in its vicinity and yet continues to have sympathy for the white settlers who were systematically destroying the lives of the people that missionaries came to serve?

It is, I fear, that in their own way, missionaries were just as driven as their white farmer counterparts to see the destruction of the "wicked heathen" cultures of people in Africa and transform them into a "Christian society."

There was a photo in the Wheaton archives of a wall plaque that appears to have hung on a missionary's wall. It is a missionary revision of a nineteenth-century hymn. It was set inside a frame in the shape of Africa. The first lines of verse say:

I know of a land that is sunk in shame,
Of hearts that faint and tire.

The second stanza begins:

The restless millions wait
The light there dawning
Make all things new.

The theological rat's nest of this ditty would take too many pages to untangle. But what I find most insulting is the arrogance of cultural superiority that expresses the opinion of an entire continent with "I know of a land that is sunk in shame."

Please, pray tell, what land is sunk in the most shame, the victims of its good intent or the land that would deem it noble to pen such nonsense?

I have little doubt that some sort of promise was, in fact, made to the locals of Kijabe about being a community that would be an example of unity to Africa. To the early missionaries, that simply meant that the African Christians were to Westernize. To the Africans, on the other hand, it meant and means something a little closer to what the apostle said "there be no distinctions," a model where brothers and sisters are united in the message and love of the Christ, not in a grand idea of "Western Christian culture"—a concept without credible meaning.

CHAPTER 22

TRADITIONAL AFRICAN EDUCATION

"In traditional (classical) African education there is no destination degree but rather a series of rebirths or life event stages that continue until death. Everyone is a student and a teacher at every stage. Every stage costs the student and benefits both the student and the teacher.

"Specialized training is provided at a cost in multiple disciplines as different stages are reached. There are no dropouts as life and education are inseparable. Very importantly, there is no construction of a box, with a roof, that is set aside for education. The walls are the culture and the roof is the stars."

I wrote the original draft of the above statement on traditional African education in 2011 when I was conducting research for my postgraduate degree. I remember the impact of coming to the realization of just how education in precolonial Africa differed from Western ideas of education. But it wasn't just the differences in approach, it differed in fundamental purpose.

TWO SHIFTS IN WESTERN EDUCATION

At the risk of being overly simplistic, the Western world has undergone two fundamental shifts away from its own version of traditional education.

First, the Renaissance in its various forms (Italian, English, Northern Renaissance—also known as the Reformation) often touted as the rebirth of the arts, exploration, and technology, was, in fact, the birth of the individual as separate from the society. I call this the era of the sovereign self.

Elements of this are found in what is sometimes called classical education, which involves both a methodology of learning and a body of material built around the arts, exploration, and technology.

The second shift in Western education began with the First and Second Industrial Revolutions. Independence and self-reliance were in competition with the need of industry to have a workforce (jobs).

In order to provide a workforce, the children of farmers, crafts persons, and storekeepers needed to be reoriented to seek jobs instead of putting a premium on self-reliance. The method was to have factory-style education designed to reorient children away from their parents and community and toward a better future in industry, in the form of a job. The state benefitted from the cash cow of industry and recognized the necessity of developing citizenship that was compliant to both the aims of industry and the state. From this developed the idea of a public, or factory, education. Education now moved children away from self-reliance to reliance on industry and the state.

While today's education gives lip service to the needs of a well-rounded education (code for classical education), the fact is every parent sends their child to school first and foremost to get a job—and presumably a better future. The implied contract between the parent and education is that if the parent relinquishes control to the educational system, in return this system will produce in the child the tools necessary to become gainfully employed.

The Industrial Revolution wins. The individual is no longer able to produce a means of living apart from direct or indirect participation in the workforce of the industrial machine.

The state wins. The state has established itself as the purveyor of factory education, the one who is relied on to keep unemployment under control via a placated industry. Therefore, the national unemployment numbers become so critical to a happy citizenry. And the system falls apart if there is little or no industry available for the industry-trained workforce to find employment.

The high percentage of wealth that has been gained by dropouts of the educational system should be a hint that creativity and independence is crushed by factory education.

FACTORY EDUCATION

Factory education looks like a factory. A sufficient quotient of children is separated from their parents and placed for a predetermined amount of time into a building designed like a factory—or fish farm or cattle farm. Separated by age, they are taught a prescribed amount of information. When they have sufficiently obtained the prerequisite information, they are moved to a different room where additional information is obtained. This continues until they are qualified to leave that building and move to another building for additional information. This continues for about twelve years. After twelve years, they are qualified to begin a minimal job in the industrial machine. It almost doesn't matter what the content of the education is. The form (factory education) does more to inform the actual outcome of this education than does the content. Even so-called classical education has submitted now to the factory system.

As the face of industry changes, the recipients are not qualified for much beyond the minimal ability to get a minimal job. The graduates do not appreciate or understand an investment, the basis of business, economics, or the various theories of self-reliance. They do not even understand how to think in any real creative way.

Of course, they all have learned creative and critical thinking, and not surprisingly, they all think in similar creative ways. They only understand a dualistic world (left and right—a political construct designed by the state). They know little more than to pick a side and stick with it. They are not realistically trained to understand a multiple of other alternatives to the left and the right.

Whatever qualifications they may have earned about how to function or thrive in the culture were picked up outside of the educational factory. The factory education is not there to make them critical thinkers or self-reliant. It is there to make them compliant workers, dependent on the state, so to maintain low unemployment numbers.

I highly recommend that those who have not done so look up Sir Ken Robinson, who has given TED talks on changing education paradigms. His animated talks, which among other things demonstrate factory education, can easily be found on YouTube.

Understand this. Modern education is designed to create a workforce, not industry. For most of the world, which does not have a strong industrial basis, this type of education is cruel and unsustainable.

SIDEBAR—UNIVERSITIES

University education, in theory, is a different creature. Though universities, too, are quickly becoming factory education in much of the Western world. The idea of universities and specialization existed long before the Western world crept into existence. Universities in their purest form, as far as I can tell, began in various regions of Africa.

They have been a part of African education for several thousands of years at least.

LET'S PRETEND

Now pretend for a moment that highly trained factory-education teachers go to a place—a special place in Africa where they have been convinced of a need, somewhere where these well-intentioned teachers want to set up factory education for the natives so they can better themselves. Armed with the belief that education is the key to freedom from oppression, these teachers begin a tradition of factory education in that designated place in Africa.

But there is one key ingredient missing for factory education to succeed in this special part of Africa. That missing ingredient is their own industrial revolution. The promise of the factory education is that the child put in the system will be better prepared for the emerging world. But the promise is based on a false premise because there must first be an industrial complex to provide jobs for the thousands of young people pushed through the factory-educational system.

Factory education does not and cannot produce industry. It can only produce workers for industry. If there is no industrial complex already in place looking for these factory students, the result is simple—massive unemployment and truly angry desperate young people who can neither move into the industrial workforce nor return to their traditional self-reliant past.

How I wish that we were just pretending.

I, for one, am not a fan of the Industrial Revolutions, nor am I a fan of the modern factory-educational system. I am not implying that Africa needs to have or not have an industrial revolution of its own. That is up to Africans, not me. But I am saying that exporting Western education through factory education is massively destructive.

Now African countries have constructed their own factory-educational systems. It is in the African governments' interests to operate factory education because factory education produces compliant and dependent citizens. This is a primary source of power for any government. It is not what is in the best interests of the citizens, it is a matter of what is in the best interest of the state.

Another benefactor of factory education in places like Kenya, is neocolonialism. With the suppressed workforce, Western operations and manufacturing plants benefit from the cheap workforce brought about by high unemployment. This type of unsustainable education fosters dependency on overseas interests.

TRADITIONAL AFRICAN EDUCATION

Traditional African education, like any system of education, can absorb and add any aspect of modern thinking that it deems valuable to its culture. The African system does not stunt learning. It is the opposite of Western civilization because it does not begin with the premise of the sovereignty of the individual over the culture. It does not train its people to get jobs, but it does not preclude such a thing either. It gives far more freedom than does a factory education. Freedom to think. Freedom to produce and live apart from working for another person or industry. Freedom to enter debate on the merits of an argument alone without resorting to polarity arguments—produced by the state.

How dare anyone, especially the missionary, seek to educate another culture. Western educators know only factory education. There is no instruction in the sacred writings of Christianity that gives liberty to bring education to another culture. In fact, education, as popularly conceived, is not in view at all in the texts. Factory education subdues and destroys culture, and it promotes a version of the

Christ that cannot be separated from industry and the state. This is a false gospel.

I would, however, dare one to consider which idea of education, traditional African or Western factory, is closer to what is taught in the scriptures: The one that encourages one to be an individual apart from the community or the one that sees the individual as an inseparable part of the community? The one that separates the child from the parent and community and puts them on a path of no return or the one that never separates anyone ever from interdependence in community?

Every page of the sacred texts that missionaries claim to believe in promotes community, unity, and interdependence. This same community, unity, and interdependence is the essence of traditional African education, the opposite of Western Education.

There is no contest as to which educational system is superior. Traditional African education has begun no major or world wars; disrupted the lives and cultures of none; does not depend on industrialization or the power of state; depends instead on the function of the community as a whole; does not offer a job as an outcome—not a wage, but a life.

In a very real sense, traditional African education offers life in community. Factory education, on the other hand, offers little more than a struggle just to survive. The human was designed to function in community. The loneliness, suicide rate, and aberrant behavior of the West can directly be contributed to factory education—the sickness of individualism over community. The true crime is that, now, the colonialized world is experiencing these same symptoms for the same reason.

Western education is one of the most destructive forces on earth, and missionaries are the spearhead for it across the globe.

CHAPTER 23

COMPLEXITY

I well remember, in anthropology classes at the university, listening to lectures about the evolution of complexity in societies. Offhand, I can't remember all the stages, but the idea went something like this.

And before I explain, please understand that I disagree with the opening idea that there is such a thing as a primitive society, and I disagree that so-called primitive societies are based on simple structures. But this is what I was taught in anthropology.

Primitive societies, the anthropologists teach, have simple social structures. Beginning as egalitarian hunter-gather communities, they become more complex as they develop councils of the elderly. From that, tribal communities develop, then comes chiefdoms, then expansionism. Expansionism turns into territorial wars, which lead to feudalism and eventually states or countries.

This progression in civilization, of course, is a lesson in the stages of Western civilization. The assumption behind it is that with increased complexity (as seen by the West) each society becomes more sophisticated and, therefore, more progressive. This is, without doubt, a Western-centric perspective.

However, by this definition of social evolution, the African continent reached a high level of complexity several thousands of years before the West. Africa had sophisticated universities and highly

149

organized political structures—the equivalent of states. They were highly advanced in mathematics and the sciences. The West, at the same time, was comprised of warring tribal bands, enslavement, and, ultimately, a feudal system that was among the factors that locked it into a dark age.

So, the question becomes, what happened to the African continent that was so far ahead of the West? The assumption behind this question is that any reversal from the West's idea of complexity is social devolution. The West, in contrast, with its ever-increasing complexity, is considered progressive. African history does not show an advancement in complexity (at least as defined in the West) in its social evolution.

Before I address this, I will acknowledge several factors that are often offered to explain the loss of complexity, especially in sub-Saharan African civilizations. Those factors are: 1) the desertification of the Sahara, which began in earnest about 2000 BCE, creating a barrier between southern Africa and the rest of the world; 2) the disease matrix because of the prolonged proximity of humans to animals, especially large herds of domesticated animals; and 3) the slave trade of Africans to the Middle East, Far East, and the West.

Clearly, all the above have had an impact on Africa and have, no doubt, added to the struggles of modern Africa to regain its former history and dignity. I think, however, these explanations fail to address the so-called loss of complexity in a continent that, historically, was far more complex than any other place on earth. The reason these factors do not adequately explain a loss of complexity is that Africa began its move away from complexity before these factors came significantly into play.

I remember in another university class studying Romanticism and its worship of nature. The romantics saw an end to the usefulness of reason and logic. They felt that the rationalism of the West had more than proven its incapability to solve the most basic human needs. Ultimately, they saw that, unless humanity restored its relationship with nature, culture would become increasingly cruel and violent. So far, they have been proven right, in my view, and the Western culture of rationalization has had a cancerous effect on the earth.

The problem with the Romantic period (one of many) is that practitioners deified nature and, in so doing, ultimately pitted the human against the natural. In other words, they saw humanity as defiling nature and, therefore, nature must be protected from humans. By protecting nature from humans, they insured that their objective to restore humanity's relationship with nature would never, and could never, happen.

The stepchildren of the Romantic period and its deification of nature are modern-day conservationists. In order to preserve the sanctity of nature, they developed fortress conservation—a model where the natural at its best is devoid of human contact. This model has been exported all over the world by its believers with brutal force, displacing and destroying entire indigenous cultures to insure their dogmatic ideas of nature.

Pause to consider this. Name a place in the world beyond the Western world (and perhaps China) where the indigenous people were (or are) not living in harmony with nature. One might be able to pick out a couple exceptions, but humans long ago learned to live within nature in such a way that the natural world thrived. What changed was the domination of the world by the West. The one civilization that cannot live in harmony with the natural world—nor does it have any idea how to do so—is marching across the globe establishing conservation fortresses, trying to save nature as defined by a failed Romantic period.

The journey into complexity in the West has been a journey of increasing discontinuity between humanity and the nature that gives the civilization both life and breath. It is an intellectual mirage that suggests this as a progressive system of complexity.

The story of Western civilization is not a story of complexity. Rather it is a story of centralization of power and disenfranchisement, by the central powers, of those perceived to be weak.

Ancient complex civilizations in Africa, as well as the Americas and elsewhere, went in a different and far more complex direction. They moved away from ancient centralization and toward localized communal-self-sufficiency. The over two thousand languages in Africa is an indication of the triumph of its civilization not, as some have implied, its failure.

It may seem contradictory that such a diversity of language and cultures points to a unified concept of civilization. However, the fact that so many cultures coexist and have done so for over a millennium is evidence that such a unified civilization does exist. This type of coexistence could never succeed in Western ideas of civilization without centralized authority.

It is vogue to point out that Africa is a continent, not a country, and therefore using the term "African" is too vague to make any accurate generalization. Of course, prior to colonialism, there were no countries, per se, in most of Africa south of the Sahara. While this is quickly changing, even modern countries in Africa have a wide diversity of cultures within themselves. But that diversity is the essence of their unity. Most modern African scholars point to this unified civilization. They are using the term African to point to this unification with words like "Ubantu" and phrases like "I am because we are" to demonstrate this essential unified civilization. For them, there really is such a thing as African that is much broader than any description of an isolated culture or Western-constructed African country.

If one were to take away factors related to colonialism and the slave trade, Africans, despite their diversity of language and culture, are a remarkably peaceful people. The primary part of the Bantu expansions, which occurred, for the most part, between three and four thousand years ago, changed the face of Africa south of the Sahara. It accounts for much of the language diversity. Yet by all accounts, it was a remarkably peaceful event. People who wanted to live together in community did so, and people who wanted to move on did. Conflicts were very local, and anything remotely resembling war was almost unheard of.

Despite the incredible diversity of peoples, the entire continent of Africa is crisscrossed with traditional trading routes going back long before slavery. Cultures were constantly in contact and just as constantly adopting ideas from each other. All without force. As for the so-called warring cultures in Africa, they were stationed along African slave routes to keep slavery away from their own cultures. War was almost exclusively a defensive posture. The exceptions, such as Shaka Zulu, were remarkable because they were exactly that, exceptions.

For a Western state to succeed, there must be a unified center, a unified contract, and a unified culture. Otherwise there will be conflict and civil war.

In contrast, Africans have succeeded for millennia without a unified center, without a unified contract, and with one of the most diverse matrixes of cultures on earth. That is proof of the success of one hell of a complex civilization.

In the West's historical tales, the Roman Empire was, at the time of its existence, the epitome of sophistication and complexity. It took the brutish Vandals, Franks, and Goths together to conquer the more complex Romans and end, for all practical purposes, the Roman civilization. The Romans had lost their brutish edge and designed rules for war and peace. It took a less complex civilization with no regard for civility to defeat them. The same pattern is often repeated throughout history and the world. The Americans copied the Native American and fought the British army by hiding behind rocks and trees. The Americans disregarded all civility and did not choose to face the far superior British army in organized lines of conflict. Unconventional warfare is the only reasonable way to defend against a superior force.

Brutish force and sophistication are not good bedfellows. It does not follow that the culture that conquers and colonizes other civilizations by force is the most complex. It only demonstrates which one is the most brutish. Might is not right. In fact, history seems to indicate that might, by its nature, ignores right.

Whatever one thinks of the historicity of the story of the Tower of Babel, it seems that the diversity of culture and languages was the antidote against the monster of a unified civilization under a common language. One would think that those missionaries who follow the teachings of the scriptures, as sacred, would be disinclined to glorify a unified civilization with common language over and above a civilization based in a diversity of both language and culture—exactly what the divine intention was at Babel.

For the missionary, the path to spreading the gospel, as they understand it, is in the wake of the brute force of an expansionist civilization far less complex than those it conquers. In their zeal to spread a message, missionaries authenticated and legitimized a brutal colonial monster. This is true no matter their intentions.

If the God of today's missionary is so weak that the Good News of Peace on Earth must be protected by the modern-day equivalent of the Vandals and the Goths, then the God of the missionary is too weak to bother with much of anything at all.

CHAPTER 24

THE BUS

The bus was white with a red stripe down the side, the colors of the school and its sports team. It was lumbering along the bumpy road from Nairobi back to my high school in Kijabe. All but a few of us on the bus were children of missionaries. Amid the laughter and singing that rang throughout the bus, I sat and thought about what had just happened. I was not filled with the joy that seemed to be emanating from those around me. My feeling was peculiar.

I had just accomplished what, in the bubble of my missionary world, was lauded to be the epitome of a Christian's purpose on earth and what I understood at the time to be the Great Commission. I had won a soul to Christ. What I felt was a kind of guilt—almost shame.

For several days before that bus ride, we had been trained in an exciting new way of winning souls for Christ. A simple four step process called the Four Spiritual Laws.

Every fiber of my being felt that what I had done was a sham. I knew full well how Africans respond to sincerity. I knew the man who had been sitting on the streets of Nairobi was almost certainly responding to me, a *mzungu* (white) child, and not to my words and their meaning.

It would take years for me to understand what I understand now about the gospel. But back then, on that bus, the seeds of doubt were sown in me. In addition to doubting the methods of the missionary world, I began to doubt the basic missionary message itself.

CHAPTER 25

THE GOSPEL
OF CAESAR

S everal times I have mentioned directly or indirectly that what is
being taught in the mission field is a false gospel. An audacious
claim to some, I am certain. I will make a few observations that I hope
will make my claim, at least, a bit more understandable.

It seems important to understand a few things, often forgotten,
about the word "gospel."

The Gospel of the Christ is a political statement. It is not a religious message.

At least it was a political claim when it was used in the first century. Two thousand years of religious reinterpretation has chosen to
ignore this. But when the word gospel was used, at the time it was
mentioned in reference to the Christ, it was a bold and dangerously
political claim.

It was a well-known word before the birth of the Christ.

The life and story of Caesar Augustus was known as the Gospel
of Augustus, the savior of all mankind. Messengers called *ēvangelistīs*
(evangelists) were sent ahead of the approaching Roman army shout-
ing the *ēvangeliō* (gospel) that the Lord of All (Caesar) was coming
with his hosts (army). Those who changed allegiance (repented) and

accepted the lordship of Caesar would enter his peace. Those who rejected, the wrath of Caesar's hosts was upon them.

In general, the Gospel of Caesar Augustus was the rehearsed story of his miraculous birth, life, and rise to power and glory.

Of Caesar, it was said that when the "perfect time came" the Providence sent to the descendants of mankind a "Savior who put an end to war, put things in order, and fulfilled the hope of all times."

If you know even a smidgen of the life and claims of the Christ, called Jesus, you will recognize that I could almost have replaced "Augustus" and "Caesar" with "Jesus" and "Christ" and describe the claims in the scriptures of the person and works of the Christ.

Consider the audacity of the Christ who stood in the Caesar's kingdom and declared that it was He and not Caesar that was King of Kings. It was His peace, not the peace of Caesar that mattered. It was His birth and life and rise to power that mattered, not the story of a lord of this earth.

The politics of Jesus the Christ confronts the politics of this earth. But it does not do so with swords but by serving the poor in spirit, the meek, the ones who hunger and thirst. It confronts the political powers with love and a community of the disenfranchised.

At first, the disciples of the Christ made the same mistake that people who call themselves Christians make today.

When the disciples recognized that Jesus was the promised Christ, they anticipated that He would establish His long-awaited kingdom by force.

Perhaps, one of the reasons the phrase in the scriptures "at the right time, the Christ came" is used in three locations is that the idea of a gospel meant almost the same thing in both the Hebrew and Roman worlds. The coming Christ anticipated in the Hebrew texts was that of a victorious priest-king who would bring restoration and fulfill the promises made to David, Moses, Abraham, and at the fall of man in the story of Adam and Eve. In this book, I have tried to consistently refer to "the Christ" rather than simply "Christ" because the term is a title, not a name. Now, as I will explain next, I will go one step further and replace "the Christ" with "the King."

Recently, I have been reading the translation of the New Testament made by the scholar N. T. Wright called, very significantly, the Kingdom New Testament. In it, I have noticed that in the Gospels, Wright frequently uses the word "King" rather than "Christ." In fact, it was a king that the Hebrews looked forward to that would rescue their people from their oppression and establish an everlasting peace. I think that N. T. Wright captures the primary significance of the idea of "Christ" with this translation, an idea long lost in many or most of the religious dogmas and traditions of Christianity. At this point, I will follow Wright's lead and do the same for the remainder of this and, in large part, the following essays.

It is surprisingly uncomfortable to say "King" instead of "Christ" at first, but it drives home the point. Further, it becomes beautiful and makes the Kingdom very present, once one becomes used to the change in terms.

For the Romans, the gospel was found in the Pax Romana of the Caesars; for the Hebrews, the gospel was to be found in the coming of a son of David who would rule both as a priest and as a king.

Both the Romans and the Hebrews saw their gospels in terms of roaring lions that would be enforced by the only way any political system of this earth understands—with violence.

Instead, the King instructed his co-regents, "You know the rulers of this world lord it over their peoples, and officials flaunt their authority over those under them. But among you it will be different. The one who wants to be a leader among you must be your servant."

Even when the King entered Jerusalem for the last time, the disciples fully expected Him to use His powers to overthrow Roman oppression. Instead, He became a servant and washed His disciples' feet, including the feet of Judas who would betray Him. He told them to follow His example.

Very possibly, Judas was among the Zealots, and the betrayal was intended to force the hand of Jesus to lead the rebellion against their oppressors. But at the most opportune moment, when confronted by Pilot, the King said, "My kingdom is not of this world, otherwise my servants would fight." The King refused to establish His kingdom through violence.

This is not a postponed kingdom; it is a kingdom of a profoundly different nature. It is not a kingdom "like the lords of the earth" that is "here or there" because it is already among us. All of us.

The gospel is the story of the birth, life, and conquest of a king. It is not a religious message about an individual's salvation. It is not the foundation of a new religion. It makes both religion and kingdoms obsolete—while acknowledging they both exist. It is the salvation of the whole world. A salvation from the oppression of the two most dangerous "principalities and powers" on earth—religion and politics. If one chooses to be a part of this kingdom now, there is peace now. There is always trouble on this earth as it remains locked up by the twin powers, but there is freedom now for those who believe, and for all mankind in the life to come.

The Gospel of the King has no allegiance to the powers of this earth. It does not support any particular political party or position; it does not support but rather acknowledges the kings of the earth. It does not curry favor with colonial powers; it does not work on behalf of kings or, for that matter, religion. It claims the kingdoms of the earth, that we see and hear about every day, to be both defeated and irrelevant.

Yet the kings of this earth still exist. Therefore, believers are told to submit to ruling authorities. Anyone who has grown up in a country that is different from their passport country understands this. We submit to authorities because to rebel is to lose our voice for a higher purpose. Submission comes not, as it is commonly understood, from a position of weakness. We submit because we have a higher purpose than to entangle ourselves in the affairs of this world. We want to declare that the real King of Heaven has set the captives free. For this reason, for as long as it is possible, we should live at peace with all, including principalities and powers.

It bears repeating—our brand of submission comes from a position of strength and a commitment to a higher purpose.

The disciples learned to live as if Jesus, not Caesar, was King. They did not protest Roman policies, they did not picket against unjust Roman laws, they did not join rebellions. They lived, instead, as if they were under a different authority; an authority that fought injustices by being just; fought for the oppressed by binding their wounds and loving them fully. They washed each other's feet and invited others to join them in the Kingdom made without human hands. And for their efforts, most or all of them were killed by the principalities and powers prevalent where they lived.

The audacious claim of the gospel is that we have no King but Jesus.

Those aware of American history will recognize that this mantra, "We have no king but Jesus," was one of the rallying cries of the American Revolution. But the revolution came with guns, bombs, death, the establishment of enemies, and the establishment of a new government of this earth.

All this goes to prove that whoever the king of the American revolution was, it certainly was not Jesus. King Jesus said, "My kingdom is not of the earth, otherwise my servants would fight." The King announced a kingdom without borders that cannot be found on a map, that makes no distinctions—all are the children of their Creator. It is an army of servants that refuse to fight but willingly die.

It is completely understandable that people will reject the claims of a king of such an invisible kingdom, claims that the High King of Heaven makes all kingdoms and religion irrelevant—though we see both.

Those who join this kingdom live in freedom from the bondage of those powers in this life. But in the end, this freedom is for all people. That is the good news! The end of both religion and politics.

The problem is that few have had a chance to accept or reject the Gospel of the King because the gospel they hear is not about freedom. It is a message, instead, of bondage to a new system of dogma that surrounds a religion that has developed and dominated over the last two thousand years—a religion that pays treasonous homage to the principalities and powers of this earth; a religion that, in fact, often condemns most of the world to misery. It is a religion that claims to be the only true religion, a religion that reduces to mockery and absurdity the claim of "peace on earth, goodwill to all people." But this association with both religion and powers is a false gospel. And it is what is most often promoted in the mission field.

Religion and politics always get in the way of the most fundamental essence of the Gospel of the King: we really have no King but Jesus, we really have no government other than the Kingdom of Jesus, which is not built with human hands.

CHAPTER 26

PRINCIPALITIES
AND POWERS

The Gospel of the King is not the establishment of a new or improved religion. It does not build religious buildings; it does not establish dogma. It does claim that, in knowing the life and teachings of the King, one begins to see human life as the Creator intended it to be and the purposes of God toward mankind—"That they be one as we are one."

But religion thwarts this purpose and political entanglements destroy any real meaning in the message. If the world does not see the Kingdom of the King in the love and sacrifice of those who claim to be His followers, then it does not see the Kingdom of the King at all. Instead, it sees a vain and contemptuous religion that curries favor with kings and kingdoms.

A religion that defines its enemies is not a part of the Kingdom of the King.

THE GOOD SAMARITAN

Too many messages have been preached on what the Good Samaritan did instead of who the Samaritan was. The question being asked of the King was, "Who is my neighbor?" Certainly, it is important to answer this question if the second of the two greatest commandments is to "love your neighbor as yourself." The narrower one can define the circle of who is considered a neighbor then, presumably, the easier it is to love them.

Samaritans were enemies of no regard.

Jesus went to the ultimate extreme in His answer. He was saying that your neighbors are the ones that you most perceive as your enemy. A neighbor expands beyond home, neighborhood, town, and country. The King went to the most unlikely neighbor possible—a Samaritan, the longstanding enemy of Israel. Today, Jesus might as well have declared that the neighbor to be loved and the one that loved back was a Muslim, Buddhist, or Animist. Or more likely, in the United States, your neighbor is the one you would most oppose politically or theologically. The audacity of the idea that kindness would come from a Samaritan.

Until one expands their idea of neighbor to encompass the earth and all who dwell in it, they do not understand the gospel or the love of the cross. Religion subverts this and provides room for enemies. It limits neighbors to those within its circle of dogma. It aligns itself with the principalities and powers and allows the state's enemies to become its own enemies.

It is impossible to serve two masters. The Kingdom made without human hands has no enemies. It is borderless and disinterested in conquest or expansionism. The kings of this earth establish borders, protect them, and expand and exploit in their national interests. These two vastly different kingdoms are incompatible.

Religion focuses on what the Samaritan did rather than who the Samaritan was. The question of the story of the Samaritan was, "Who is my neighbor?" It was not, "What should I do to be a good neighbor?"

A Roman soldier was an enemy of high regard.

The historical animosity between the Hebrews and the Samaritans was not nearly as acute nor the crisis as immediate as the conflict between the Romans and their Hebrew subjects. If you can imagine a successful takeover of your country by a terrorist nation, then you might be able to understand the conflict in the Hebrew mind of being subjects of Rome.

The escalating crisis between the Hebrew and Romans was at a breaking point because the Romans had introduced their gods, religious symbols, and worship centers in Jerusalem. This was a defilement of the historical city that spawned winds of rebellion. It was a crisis that, after the death of Jesus, led to the Jewish Revolt and ultimate destruction of Jerusalem. The last straw was when the Romans placed objects of foreign worship in the Hebrew temple itself.

But it was a Roman soldier that the King pointed to and exclaimed that He had not seen such great faith like this in all of Israel. This was occasioned when the soldier asked the King to heal his servant. The King was at peace with the world, regardless of station or whether the world was at peace with Him.

And what is most compelling is not only the lack of enmity expressed toward the soldier but also the lack of political implication in the compassionate act of the King toward the servant of the Roman soldier. There was no suggestion that the man cease to be a soldier, even a soldier of Rome.

This same lack of political implication is found again when the King was tested for His political ideals when He was asked about the tax and if should it be paid to Caesar. This was a central issue of the rebellion and taking a side would have identified the King politically. Was He liberal or conservative, was He a progressive or a reactionary— was He really claiming to be the King who would bring redemption to a nation and save them from their enemies?

I imagine this question being asked in the modern American political climate: "King, are you for or against abortion? Do you support the interment of children at our borders? Who are you politically, which party best supports your agenda?"

"Give to government what belongs to government and to God what belongs to God."

The King was profoundly disinterested in the policies of Rome. When the policies of Rome and the Hebrew conflict caught up with Him, and He was on the verge of crucifixion, His comment was simple and utterly profound: "Father, forgive them, for they know not what they do."

"Father, forgive them, for they know not what they do."

This statement by the King as He was dying, was understood by the early Christians as a statement that covered all humans on earth. There is no rebellion or political power too great to escape this forgiveness. That is the gospel's cutting edge in the world.

Rather than being horrified by the pagan practices of the cultures they encountered, the missionaries should have marveled that the gospel covers all regardless of what they do. Instead of trying to end practices deemed un-Christian, they should have recognized that the King himself was the friend of sinners.

There is nothing they can do that separates them from the love of God. This is the end of religion, not the starting point of a new or improved one. What changes a person, when a change is needed, is the knowledge and experience of that love. It is not the onerous demand to be more chaste and more Christian.

Christianity, if it was ever a good thing, has become the essence of the kind of religion that angered the King the most. It was not the drunkard, the prostitute, the tax collector, the Samaritan, or the Roman that brought out the indignation and anger of the King, it was those who hold to their religious traditions and thereby neglect God.

Unlike the King whose Kingdom is made without hands, the Western missionary has identified the Christian faith with traditional Western values. Instead of not taking political sides in the political systems of the earth, like their King did, they affirm the Christian left or the Christian right, because they have become so entangled with the political powers of this earth that they cannot recognize the King without taking political positions.

Here I briefly go back to the article that started these essays in the first place. The remarkable success of the missionaries in the article is measured by how many societies now have better (Westernized) education and are more democratic than those who were not influenced by said missionaries. Is the gospel of education and democracy anywhere to be found in the teachings of the King?

One can only look at this success in peddling education and democracy as a good thing if they ignore the essence of the gospel. The gospel is decidedly political, but it is a political institution built without human hands. To recognize any other political consequence as a success is to admit that the gospel of those missionaries is, in fact, not the Gospel of the King. It is instead far more like the Gospel of Caesar, who believed that by benevolent force and conquest he could bring peace to the world. The democracy of the missionary is no less monstrous than the Pax Romana of Rome.

As I have said before, I have little doubt about the accuracy of the studies behind the article about the relationship of missionaries and the rise of democracy and literacy in the world—but this is evidence of abysmal failure not success.

Better it would be to say, "Give to the chief, or the elders, or the king what belongs to them and give to God what belongs to God, and take no heed of the systems of this world."

Better to love without recognizing distinctions—no enemies, no progressives, no conservatives, no slaves, no free, no gays, no lesbians, no transgenders, no Christians, no Muslims, no Buddhists, no agnostics, no atheists, no Klansmen, no al Qaeda, no terrorists (Christian, Muslim, or otherwise), no racists, no presidents, no governors, no communists, no socialists, no capitalists, no to all distinctions.

While I do not find a compelling argument for the role of a missionary in the teachings of the King, if there is to be one, it must be a role that makes no distinctions, that loves without conditions, and that lets the Caesars be Caesars.

CHAPTER 27

HOPE

In Greek mythology, Pandora's box explains the human condition in a story of an angry Zeus who devises a punishment for a lesser god, Epimetheus, for freeing his brother from Zeus's chains. Zeus creates a woman named Pandora and gives her the gifts of wisdom, beauty, generosity, health, and everything desirable to a Greek god. But she is also created to be curious. Epimetheus falls in love with her and marries her despite warnings of the trickery of Zeus.

As a wedding present, Zeus gives Pandora a beautiful box but warns her never to open it. Curiosity overwhelms Pandora, and she opens the box. All the misery of human experience flies out of the box, war, hunger, pain, disease, and death among them. Pandora slams the box shut, but it is too late. All but one misery has escaped the box. A voice inside the box begs Pandora to let it escape too. Pandora listens and finally opens the box one more time. Hope escapes into the world.

Ever since Pandora, humans have endured misery by holding on to hope.

Mythology, like all ancient tales, has many layers of lessons. For some, hope is seen as the one thing that allows humans to survive the misery of life. For others, hope is the cruelest gift of all, because instead of resisting the cause of the misery, hope creates complacency and submission.

Throughout history, each time the colonial aggressors showed up on the shores of their expanding empire, they unleashed their own box of cruel misery upon their victims that exacerbated all human suffering. They unleashed endless war, pain, disease, and the stench of suffering and death rose over it all.

There is one more component that has always came in the colonial box, the missionary. From the missionary comes the most miserable gift of all—hope. Inextricably tied to the colonial invasion, this cruel version of hope gave the basis for compliance and submission to colonialism and dulled the human capacity to stand up and resist. And its dulling effects have lingered beyond colonialism, becoming its own self-fulfilling bondage.

I am not speaking against hope itself but the kind of hope that is caught up with a box of misery.

Missionaries—indeed, much of modern Christianity—need to study a completely different type of hope, a hope not born from colonialism and Western religious tradition, a hope, instead, that is reflected solely in the revolutionary message of the King.

Hope is central to the thinking of a follower of the King. The idea of hope, however, has gone through some significant changes as different theological schools of thought have developed.

By taking a brief look at two theological shifts among American believers, I think we can see two problematic views of hope. The second shift has directly affected the missionary method and message.

In early European America, the Puritan Hope was a driving force in the colonies. Central to the Puritan Hope was the idea that America was the new promised land of God, and the various colonies developed laws and patterns of expansionism as they sought to bring about a very physical and earthly kingdom of God on earth.

This hope of the old Puritans resulted in a very proactive engagement with the here and now. Sadly, but not unexpectedly, many of the atrocities in early European American history were motivated directly by their hope that this new kingdom of God would be established in a very earthly and physical way in the New World. The Native Americans were too often seen as the Philistines that needed to be driven out or destroyed in order to establish the new kingdom, ordained by God.

After the Cromwell revolution ended in England, a group of thinkers, referred to sometimes as the New Puritans, came to America with an entirely different idea of American destiny. For them, reason and faith should operate separately. Government should be guided by reason, and moral character should be guided by faith. This idea fostered the American Revolution, which resulted, eventually, in the Constitution, which created a precarious wedge between reason and faith.

For the believers in early America, this created a crisis in their hope. It seemed that the possibility of a kingdom of God being established in an earthly and physical America was over. For a period, there was no new theological matrix with which to define a believer's hope in post-Revolutionary America.

For many, especially the more conservative believers, the problem was solved with a new idea of hope that became popularized during the so-called Second Great Awakening. No longer was hope in the here and now, hope became a waiting or postponement for the life hereafter. Devotees of this idea of postponement clung on to various scattered texts to assure them that this world was going to hell in a handbasket, but they would be the remnant that would find hope in the life hereafter.

Hope, then, was for a future not a present life. The obligation of a believer became highly individualistic, assuring their own hope individually and trying to get as many others to focus on that future hope as possible.

This same idea of hope became the rallying cry of the modern missionary movement. The logic was that if they did not go and preach the gospel and get people saved from this earth, then millions would be dammed to eternal torment.

The missionary movement is the epitome of the idea of postponed hope. The world, in this view, is full of heathens writhing on the brink of hell unless they hear the gospel and decide for salvation. No matter what the cost, the missionary feels compelled to save the lost from eternal flames.

Obviously, there really is a future hope in a believer's life that extends beyond the grave. But the force of hope in the believer's life is to be very much, as the Puritans believed, in the here and now. It is a revolutionary hope with a very present King and Kingdom. The King was a political revolutionary with an entirely different kind of kingdom built on an entirely different set of principles.

The error of the Puritan Hope was that it intended to bring about a very physical kingdom—the same error that has always existed in much of what is called Christianity.

The major focus of hope in much of the history of American religion—both hope in a physical earthly kingdom brought about by force and the idea of a hope that is primarily postponed until the afterlife—has had dangerous and, dare I say, evil consequences.

The King said His kingdom is neither "here or over there" but that it is "already in or among you." One need only read the parables of the King that begin with "The Kingdom of God is like—" to see that the Kingdom is something very much on earth and not in some postponed alternate reality. One only needs to read the Sermon on the Mount and the instructions on authority to understand that this is a kingdom of service, love, and humility. It is brought about by neither force nor manipulation but rather love of enemies instead of war.

The Puritans tried to bring about their version of hope at the hot end of a musket, and modern missionaries flaunted their message from the front ranks of colonial expansionism.

Neither of these reflects the King who washed the feet of His disciples, including the feet of the one who was about to betray Him, with the instructions that He was giving them an example of what they should do for each other.

It is not a kingdom of force, nor is it a kingdom brought about by the threat of hellfire. It is a kingdom of love and service. If it is not seen in the love of God's people, then it is not seen at all.

The sine qua non of the so-called Lord's prayer is found in the phrase "on earth as it is in heaven."

That the King said to Pilot, "My kingdom is not of this world, otherwise my servants would fight," is one of many telling indications that the Kingdom is brought about by love to the point of sacrificing one's own life for both friend and enemy. It is not a kingdom of violence, nor does it demand violence.

There are many consequences to misplaced hope in a believer's life, one of which leads to the justification of violent means to obtain the salvation of the lost. Another is that because of misplaced hope, there is often an abandonment of responsibility for the care of this earth. Believers thinking that this world is lost to inevitable destruction do not stand shoulder to shoulder with those who have concern for the vessel of earth that gives us life. No one should be more concerned with the state of the earth than an individual who believes that the earth exists at the hands of the Creator of All Things and that the Creator called this creation good.

I am not a fan of much of what is called environmentalism or conservation, because I think the motives within these movements are heavily political and, therefore, suspect. But I believe that living the prayer "on earth as it is in heaven" includes the preservation of this earth that the Creator called good. That should be among the paramount concerns of the Kingdom on earth as it is in heaven.

It seems crucial to recognize the revolutionary figure of hope for this world that the King demonstrated. He won His battles by laying down His life and called us to do the same. His hope makes obsolete all religious and political strongholds in a believer's life.

This hope affects us and the present world we live in, not just the future. We look for an earth in which there is peace because there are no enemies that have escaped the love of the King demonstrated in us. The King is our political platform. We need no other.

This is our hope and our entire expectation: "Your will be done, on earth as it is in heaven."

CHAPTER 28

AS YOU ARE GOING

Recently, I received a sincere message from a young missionary. She asked me, if there were no missionaries, how could we carry out the Great Commission?

I will spare the nonreligious reader the entire context of this statement by the King, except to say that the phrase "go into the world and make disciples" (variously translated) is called by some the Great Commission. (Matthew 28:16-20 and Mark 16:14-18)

This question took me back just a little. I well remember how an older generation of missionaries used to say that their calling was in response to the Great Commission, and churches sent support so that they too could join in fulfilling this commission. The assumptions contained in this perspective have always been a bit staggering and filled with rather inflated views of the role of the missionary.

As with many children of missionaries, I experienced traveling to various churches scattered around America on what was known in the missionary world as "deputation." This word had a specialized nuance for many missionary societies. It was a time when missionaries would present their work to various churches back home (home to the missionaries, not so much their children). The purpose, beyond presenting needs in their chosen mission field, was to raise the funds necessary to return and continue or begin their work.

Predominantly displayed in the front of nearly every missionary-minded sanctuary was a version of the Great Commission. In general, it is from these types of churches that missionaries are sent, and it is these types of churches that missionaries visit to raise funds for their work. No wonder, then, that the young missionary asked the question, because the Great Commission is such a fundamental part of the church's missionary culture from which most missionaries evolve.

What may surprise many who live in the missionary world is that most believers have never heard of a Great Commission, and of the ones who have heard of it, few know where it comes from. None of the verses quoted in the Gospels mention the term "great commission," unless some English translator has chosen to insert the term as a heading to the passage or passages.

In my view, title insertions in English translations of scripture serve little useful purpose beyond adding needless confusion.

An interesting little book by Barbara Becker-Cantraino, *Migration and Religion*, indicates, as do other historians, that the term "the Great Commission" was created in the mid-sixteen hundreds by a Lutheran nobleman, Justinian von Welz, who was trying to convince representatives at the Imperial Diet in Regensburg to retake grounds that Lutherans had lost by promoting a revival of Lutheranism and discipleship. He headed his arguments with "The Great Commission of Jesus Christ to the Protestants." This seems to be the first use of the term and, ironically, he was seeking support, both theological and political, for his own idea of missionary zeal.

So the term itself, along with the missionary world, both have origins in political and religious cooperation. All of history is a process of ideas, and something is not legitimate only if it comes out of the first century. Neither is it in error if it comes out of the sixteenth century. However, the origins of the idea of a Great Commission come from a place and time that converged with religious and political relationships that most modern conversion Protestants would find suspicious.

What I find most ironic, however, is that while the missionary world looks to the sayings of Jesus to justify missionary endeavors, they have yet to look to the teachings of Jesus to see what instructions the followers of the King had in spreading the good news of the Kingdom of God—when you go, take nothing with you.

Personally, I find it contextually improbable that when the King spoke those words about going into the world that some sort of Great Commission was contemplated at all. If it was, it seems equally improbable that it was intended to reach beyond the disciples who heard it directly. But I am going to assume, for the sake of argument, that there is, at least in principle, an application of this text for contemporary believers.

Greek scholars have pointed out that most English translations are mistaken when they insert the imperative "go" into the phrase "go into the world and make disciples." Rather than "go," the imperative in the sentence is "make disciples."

The entire force of the so-called Great Commission, in contrast, is on a poorly translated "go," which would be better rendered "as you are going."

Considering the baggage that missionaries take with them to the mission field, it would appear that making disciples is secondary at best.

This shift from "make disciples" to "go," I think, is reflective of modern conversion Protestants' ideas of hope, discussed earlier. The objective is more on the salvation of the lost and less on the advancement of the Kingdom of God "on earth as it is in heaven." The Kingdom of God is the only useful context of discipleship and the community that develops around it.

Without a realized hope in this life, the Great Commission might as well be: "Go into the world and get the lost saved before they go to burn forever in hell." That, of course, is not what the statement of the King implies.

Hudson Taylor, an early missionary to China, famously stated about his own calling, "For me to go is China." This has become the blueprint of most missionary efforts. One who is *called* determines where to *go*.

However, since it is in the passive—"as you are going"—there is no command to go at all, but rather, the instruction is to disciple within the normal life of being human—as you are going.

Sometimes by virtue of vocation, or by extreme circumstances such as famine or war, people are naturally going throughout the world. It is in the context of life that one is to make disciples. It is not an instruction to a specialized occupation. Going is organic; it is the making disciples that is imperative.

This is what happened in the first few centuries of believers. At first, many early believers huddled around the Jerusalem area. It was persecution that sent them scattering to other parts of the Roman world. But as they were going, they made disciples. It was organic, circumstantial, or phenomenal, as with Philip and the Ethiopian eunuch (I'll spare the nonreligious the details, but you should look it up if you're interested—Acts 8).

The point is this. Those in the generations closest to the teachings of the King did not take it upon themselves to organize mission societies or start schools or build religious buildings. They were simply but profoundly disciples of the King, and they made disciples everywhere they went. It is not a profession. It is a preoccupation of a believer.

One thing obviously missing from the imperative in the statement of the King about making disciples is any intention that it be carried out as a profession, such as by missionaries. This is simply not there. It is either given exclusively to the 12 to 120 or so disciples who were there or it is prophetic about the generation of the King or it is to all believers throughout all ages. But none of these options assume a professional occupation, let alone financial support and gain for such an occupation.

The role of missionaries is an assumption of history, not a directive from the King. Whatever the intention of the words of the King, they were not, in context, a call for missionaries, since no such thing existed until centuries later—the idea of a Great Commission took a full sixteen centuries to make its debut.

So, if the "go" in the Great Commission is not intended to be understood as an imperative, it is not written for or about missionaries. This, in my view, is especially important to understand. It is no small thing to take a command of God and obey it within the traditions of men. Just ask Jesus.

I think the best illustration of the "as you are going" passage might be found in the so-called creation mandate in the book of Genesis, which says, "Be fruitful and multiply and fill the earth." The Creator of all created and sanctioned sex and made it such a compelling and beautiful need of our humanity. And not just humanity; reproduction and replication are an essential process of all living things. The fulfillment of the creation mandate is written in the sexual drive of humans. Humanity obeys the mandate without regard to their religion or lack thereof. It is fulfilled because it is written in the DNA of being human.

While there are many exceptions where wonderful and loving humans are not driven specifically by this desire, the rule still rules, and little humans are perennially born.

The King, in my view, is giving a new creation mandate. In other words, it is written in the hearts of believers. Our life is our sermon, our gatherings are our witness, our love of neighbors and enemies is our outreach to the nations—the fulfillment of the King's mandate to make disciples is written in the hearts of His people.

Of one thing we can be certain. This text of "as you are going" is a conversation between the King and His immediate disciples. At a minimum, this is instruction to them about their task as His immediate witnesses. The end of the age that He speaks of is, at a minimum and perhaps limited to, the specific age as prophesied and completed in the final destruction of the temple in 70 AD.

I have no objection to those who limit the intent of the text to those specific disciples of the King. They have the best exegesis on their side. If the passage or passages have intentions beyond the immediate disciples to whom the words were spoken, then perhaps it can be understood in a generalist way as well, the general way that all followers of the King have in their spiritual DNA the message of the gospel. It is not a profession; it is the beautiful desire that is worked out in the lives of all believers in the King, the Christ, as they are going about their lives.

The occupation of missionary is nowhere demanded in the sacred texts, especially not in the so-called Great Commission, which is the text upon which the modern missionary occupation almost entirely depends.

I don't know how well my response was received by the young missionary who asked about the Great Commission. However, in my view, she was carrying a burden that is not necessary and not part of any instruction by Jesus the Christ. It is an instruction, instead, of religious tradition.

CHAPTER 29

TAKE NOTHING

One of the underlining premises of these essays is that one who brings the message of the Christ should, I believe must, bring that message without any baggage. I want to make that point one last time, this time through my own experience.

I have mentioned before that in my journey as a follower of the Christ, I have had times of doubt about my faith, even doubt at times that there is really anything outside this cloak of human existence, times when the arguments and perspectives of my atheist and agnostic friends have been compelling. At times, I have envied these friends because of the burden I carry, feeling a responsibility to pursue what I cannot clearly see within the finite limits of this existence, the limited space in which all my experiences occur.

There are, however, several significant touchstone events in my life that serve as reminders to me that, in the end, I can never fully deny the existence of the Creator. Perhaps the fact that I need these events, from time to time, to reassure myself is an indication of my own weakness as a follower of the Christ.

I am fully aware that others who do not believe have experiences in their own lives that serve to verify their lack of belief in a Creator. In my view, most of those events are indictments on religion itself in all its various forms, including Christianity, rather than being evidence of the existence or lack of a Creator. It is precisely because of the offence of the religious that the King indicted religion with such fiery passion during His brief tenure on this earth.

Back to my touchstone events.

One of my touchstone events I recounted briefly in an earlier chapter titled "Calling." Another I will give account for now. Recalling still more events would not seem to fulfill any purpose in this book.

Like my description of my calling, this event will further certify my insanity if it is not true. But because I cannot deny it, I am left to believe it really happened.

Even now, I am reluctant to fully describe it, but I will try to reveal just enough to make my ultimate point.

When I was nineteen, I was preparing to leave Kenya, the place of my birth and upbringing. I was soon going to leave Africa and fly to America. This impending departure was ripping my heart out, as it has done for generations of missionary children before and after me.

During my last year in Kenya, I took several short trips to places that had personal significance to me as sort of a final farewell. My last trip was to northern Kenya, to a place called Log Logo, where a small mission station existed among the Rendille people in what was called, at the time, the Kaisut Desert.

Toward the end of that trip, I found myself sitting in a circle of elders, a day's drive or so from Log Logo, in a very remote part of the desert.

I was there by a series of unplanned circumstances that involved the saving of the life of a Rendille elder. My role was small. Saving the elder's life required a fast and dangerous drive through the brutally rocky desert with no road to follow, and I was the only available driver—a journey that nearly cost all our lives. But in the end, all turned out well.

I think my role was exaggerated a bit by the other two Rendille men who went with me on the trip. The elders who invited me to the circle, it seemed, intended to honor me for my role in saving the life of their fellow leader.

As part of their honoring ceremony, the Rendille handed me a stick, sometimes called a rungu in Swahili. It was, for them, a ceremonial stick. Later, I learned that the word "Rendille" roughly translates to "the holders of the stick of God." So, it seems a ceremony with a special kind of rungu had unique significance in their culture. They also told me that they were going to call me Rungu in honor of what I had done.

Though I have never again seen the Rendille, and those elders have long since gone to their ancestors, that honor and name is a treasure of my earthly life. And I still have the rungu they gave me in my possession.

More specifically to the touchstone event: I knew English and could manage in Swahili, so the two men who took the harrowing journey with me translated the elder's words to me and my words to the elders.

One of the elders began a discussion of the missionaries and why they were on the Rendille lands. At this time in my life, as I mentioned in the first chapter of this book, I was having doubts about the whole missionary machine and tiptoed through this topic. At one point, probably in response to something I said, one of the elders asked me, "Who is God?" A surprising question from an African. In those days, the assumption of a Creator of All things was fundamental to every African culture.

I was not certain how to answer. For a person of faith, the Creator is a presupposition, and beyond shadows reflected on the wall of a cave, as Plato described it, there is little that can be said with certainty. I began to answer to the best of my young mind's ability. As I spoke,

I began to realize that I was saying things that I had never known or even thought of before. I learned more about the Creator by listening to the words that were coming out of my own mouth than I have learned in a lifetime since. Some of those things are reflected in this book. It felt more than surreal.

I soon realized that the two translators had stopped translating what I was saying to the Rendille elders, but they continued to translate what the Rendille were saying as they responded to my words.

Afterwards, I asked the translators why they had stopped translating what I said. They told me that when I was speaking of the Creator, I was speaking perfect Rendille, and the elders understood every word. I expressed my shock and doubt, and the translators scolded me, saying that if my words were truly from the Creator, I should not be surprised.

I must hasten to add that I am horrible with languages. My editors will verify that I am not so good at English, either. While I have had other phenomenal experiences in my life, that single event is the only time that my words were heard in a language that I did not know and could not speak. So, I make no claim of a special gift for languages.

I have thought about that moment throughout my life, wondering what, if any, lesson I can or should take away from it. I think in reflection that this event has something in common with all the other phenomenal God encounters in my life.

I had nothing to offer. I could not practice medicine. I was not there to bring education or provide clean water. In all honesty, my motives were a bit selfish. I was among the Rendille because I loved being around them. They had such a wonderful sense of humor. And their practical jokes were hilarious—despite the fact I was often the brunt of the joke. I loved them, and I loved being around them.

It was a moment when I was living, though not by intention, as the King instructed His disciples when He sent them out.

I took nothing with me.

I did not have silver or gold. I did not even have a change of clothing. The only item I had was the rungu, which the elders gave me. I was welcomed, so I stayed, but I did not stay long.

I used to think that the instruction by the King to take no extra clothing or money was simply so that a disciple would have nothing to offer but the love of the King. I now think that a secondary and equally important reason was so the believer would not be tempted to stay too long.

As I wrote and shared these essays in preparation for this book, the comment that I have received the most has been that I can't just criticize the missionary movement if I do not offer a credible alternative.

In my view, I have been addressing my answer to this critique in every essay but let me summarize it one last time.

Don't go; just be. Be a follower of the teachings of the King. As you are going about your life, linger where you are welcome, and leave where you are not. Let the love of the King compel you—most especially to love your enemies, all of them.

Live a life with nothing to offer except your passion to love as the King loved and forgive as the King forgave. Let the King build His kingdom on His own terms. Let the works of the Creator, alone, be the basis of the phenomenal events in your life.

Most importantly of all, take nothing with you.

ABOUT THE AUTHOR

Skeeter Wilson was born in Kenya, along the edge of the Gikuyu highlands, during the last years of colonialism. The son of American missionaries, he witnessed Kenya's birth pangs as it gained a semblance of independence. He spent his formative years divided between his Gikuyu friends and the children of missionaries at an American-curriculum boarding school

Wilson earned his postgraduate African History and Creative Writing degrees while doing field research in the highlands of Kenya where he grew up.

His published works include *Worthless People*, *Crossing Rivers*, and *Escape from Stupid*. He has published short stories in several traditional and online magazines.

Take Nothing With You is Wilson's debut nonfiction work.

Wilson now lives in Auburn, Washington, with his wife Jacque. Together they host guests in their treehouse, put on small writers conferences, and host an annual event called the Goat N' Guzzle, which focuses on cuisine from various cultures in Africa.

The biggest miracle in Skeeter Wilson's life has been his marriage and journey of adventures with Jacque.

APPENDIX 1

READING LIST

Here is a list of books that were recommended to me about neo-colonialism and its effects in Africa. I hope there will be those of you who are willing to open yourselves to a different reality. In their own ways, these are all good books and worth reading.

- *The Big Conservation Lie*, John Mbaria and Mordecai Ogada

- *Dead Aid*, Dambisa Moyo

- *White Man's Game*, Stephanie Hanes

- *The State of Africa*, Martin Meredith

- *How Europe Underdeveloped Africa*, Walter Rodney

- *Black Africa*, Cheikh Anta Diop

- *The Myth of Wild Africa*, Jonathan S. Adams

- *Wizard of the Crow*, Ngugi wa Thiong'o

- *Secure the Base*, Ngugi wa Thiong'o

- *The Challenge for Africa*, Wangari Maathai

- *Half of a Yellow Sun*, Chimamanda Adichie

- *Lords of Poverty*, Graham Hancock

- *A Brief History of Slavery: A New Global History*, Jeremy Black

- *Wretched of the Earth*, Frantz Fanon

APPENDIX 2

WHAT DO YOU THINK OF MISSIONARIES?

I put out a simple survey question to Kenyans in October of 2018. I encourage all to read these responses. This is one of the countries that supposedly benefited from independent Protestant missionaries. I invite you to imagine what these respondents would say about the article referred to throughout the text. This is a fair reflection of the range of what I heard in my interviews. Here is the question and some of the answers (with some minor edits for readability).

"IF YOU ARE A KENYAN, TELL ME HONESTLY AND SUCCINCTLY WHAT YOU THINK OF MISSIONARIES IN KENYA."

- He-he-he! Right! Remind me again who is a missionary.

- Single most successful story ever witnessed in Kenyan history. May missionaries be blessed for their work in this country of transforming lives.

- Are there any missionaries left in Kenya? I thought they all boarded flights back to their home country?? Am shocked.

- They are buried in Kenya.

- They "fertilized" Kenyan soils ...

- Also does a missionary have to be white? Or can anyone be a missionary?

- When I was a boy, a Canadian family had settled at my home place, and learned the local lingua. Their presence rather puzzled me. What made them come so far from their home, to teach us about Jesus? How did they feel? Weren't their children put to too much trouble, going learning (what school? home?). Didn't they miss home? I find those are the same thoughts I still have of the missionary.

- I went to Catholic missionary schools. It was strict, but I appreciate the work they do. Compared to other nonprofit institutions, they take their work of education and health seriously.

- I marvel at the selflessness of some missionaries, but I feel that religion serves the Western ruling elite and advances their interests especially to create markets and extract natural resources without resistance from the natives. The missionaries either know this or don't. I suspect most do.

- Truthfully, this question has been bothering me. Having grown up around missions and missionaries, and seen the good and bad, I think a serious redefining is needed. What is a missionary? What is their mission, vision, core values? This is another Africa. (Isaiah 55:11)

- Let me not give an honest answer …

- My take is that they were used to soften the Africans' hearts to submission, which gave the colonizers an easy time to reign over us.

- They had a dual conflicting role, to soften and confuse Africans (which is the general role of Xianity, to mush up the human soul). But missionaries were also our educators, and Xianity has played a huge role in the development of science, e.g., Gregor Mendel.

- Missionaries are the projectors of soft power of a culture. They shape ideals and values through missionary work. That's all I know about missionaries; they exhibit savior mentality hence colonialism.

- I have a conflicted appreciation (with a healthy dose of criticism) of the missionaries role in the early days of the trek toward building a "Nation State"—faltering as the journey has been. Those often well-meaning people played both positive and inadvertently negative roles …

- The soft invisible powers and incentives of capitalism that complement the hard powers of the gun in an injustice creation operation that capitalism creates in every new frontier it creates. It is the product of missionary (submission) that maintains capitalism for its unjustified existence. I wonder how black people can be either Christians or capitalists. Or maybe I don't have to wonder because it is for the same reasons the invaders of black civilization had to rob black civilization from its natural resources, cultural identity and make them serve the interests of the Caucasian civilization with

two weapons, capitalism without a human face and missionary weapons of mental enslavement.

- Some were double agents doing missionary work during the
day while joining their gun-totting colleagues in the dark to
flush out freedom fighters. The Chinese are doing the same
by laying groundwork through massive infrastructure projects to create new markets for their goods and shipping back
raw material.

- Missionaries came as bitter people and left their bitterness
in us through borderline differences, clannism/tribalism,
corruption, and a divided nation through creation of social
classes. In a nutshell, missionaries are to be blamed for our
situation now!

- Just make a visit to a town called Kijabe in Kiambu county
and witness firsthand missionaries with a wall built round
them. Get back and define the term missionary.

- Many of them are sincere, selfless human beings who believe
they make the world a better place through the preaching and
teaching of the Gospel of Jesus Christ. Some people know
they did/do, while there are those who do not trust them,
their mission, and how it all began.

- I think they start off from a good, moral place, and I cannot deny that Catholic missionaries for many years were the
mainstay of education and medical care in northern Kenya.
However, I cannot deny that once they get here, there is an
aspect of self-actualization or aggrandizement in their work.
Then there is their historical role in colonization. Many

missionaries are good, helpful people, but today, we must ask ourselves: what is their mission?

- Missionaries are humble people popularizing the message of Christ all over the world. In Kenya they shared the gospel, planted churches, built schools, and established hospitals. They are still here, probably in as many numbers as before, doing noble projects in remote parts of our world where most of us probably wouldn't feel comfortable enough to serve.

- Men and God's mission.

- After 53 years on ... Are they "relevant" in Kenya? Hasn't the country heard enough about one Jesus Christ—who has not helped the country in the last half a century?

- Missionaries have been the other, softer and more appealing, face of colonialism, neocolonialism, and exploitation of people in Africa. Every human being (even the most evil) have their goodness/good side and evil, vengeful side ... (for instance, Hitler loved a woman) ... but can we judge Josef Stalin from the sweet, loving letters he wrote to his wife, Tatochka, or by the fact that he killed 20 million people? If missionaries softened the path for the entry and entrenchment of colonial evils (i.e., gross violations of human rights, murder, rapes, robbery of our lands and resources, etc.) and if they rubbished and equated our spirituality with satanism ... why should we not associate them with the evil committed here? Did these "holy" people ever oppose or condemn (is there evidence of this) the evils committed against Kenyans in the colonial period?

- Frankly, I support our older people who said: "Gutiri mut-hungu na mubia" (i.e., There's no difference between the colonialist and the white missionary). Plus, again, why did the missionaries find it necessary to equate European culture with Christianity? I am not sure what missionaries do today, but all I know is that the exploitation they started here is now so well entrenched (we have "supermarkets" that sell miracles; ultra-rich clergy; a Catholic church that has organized all its faithful into jumuias (neighborhoods) that are largely about fund-raising, etc.) ... Today, our people are torn between two worlds. On the one hand, they are adherents to an alien spirituality that is more about the European culture than anything else, while on the other hand, they still cling to certain aspects of the African cultures (e.g., private consultative sessions with people rubbished as wizards/witches; love for polygamy and mpango wa kando; secretly married Catholic priests; a big and growing segment of the population that has little regard for Christian values, etc.). In a word, we would have been better off dealing with the gun-wielding colonialist and his home-guard sidekicks than dealing with them as well as the men/women who kept telling us to give the other cheek after being slapped ... this is what they still do ... they steal (and have kept stealing) our resolve to fight against what has kept us down even as they lead conflicted lives! We do not need them.

- Missionaries are the devils themselves.

- The Papalship, slavery, colonialism, and neoliberal neocolonialism in the world: my perception and how they are winning the battle for the struggle of our minds in my mind.

A movement to revoke the Papal Bull "Inter caetera" was initiated by the Indigenous Law Institute in 1992. At the Parliament of World Religions in 1994, over sixty indigenous delegates drafted a Declaration of Vision.

It reads, in part:

> We call upon the people of conscience in the Roman Catholic hierarchy to persuade Pope John II to formally revoke the Inter Cetera Bull of May 4, 1493, which will restore our fundamental human rights. That Papal document called for our Nations and Peoples to be subjugated so the Christian Empire and its doctrines would be propagated. The U.S. Supreme Court ruling Johnson v. McIntosh 8 Wheat 543 (in 1823) adopted the same principle of subjugation expressed in the Inter Cetera Bull. This Papal Bull has been, and continues to be, devastating to our religions, our cultures, and the survival of our populations.

Now that the Holy Father incoming to Sweden, and this great human being requested Kenyans to give their sound and honest opinion on missionaries, I cannot help but reject Christianity and demand the right to honor my Ancestors as was and is taught to us by our divine Stoic cultures. Read more: https://www.manataka.org/page155.html. [Link provided by respondent.]

- Missionaries prey on the poor, the illiterate. Yes, they could help them, but they fence them in.

- I can't stand their mental psychotic-bullshit acrobatics. I would throw them out of our home and let them go evangelize their sickness to their own people. What can recessive genes teach Africans: those who built mega civilizations? It's such an insult to have them here.

I organized once in our village to burn their homes, and I would do the same anytime anywhere just to have that scum of the earth out of our soil if only I had the poison that Queen Nzinga used ...

And yes, I love the bitterness displayed here, and I don't follow their god nonsense ...

For more information about Skeeter Wilson,
or to contact him for speaking engagements,
email him at *rungumzee@gmail.com*

Many voices. One message.

Quoir is a boutique publisher
with a singular message: *Christ is all.*
Venture beyond your boundaries to discover Christ
in ways you never thought possible.

For more information, please visit
www.quoir.com